wd
50
LFI
GNS

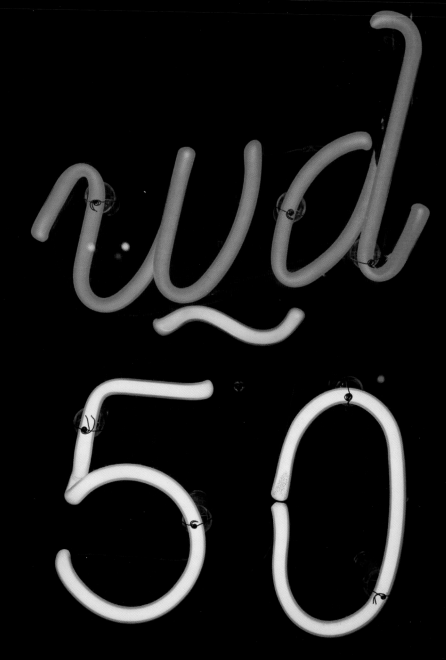

wd~50

THE COOKBOOK

WYLIE DUFRESNE

WITH PETER MEEHAN

PHOTOGRAPHY BY ERIC MEDSKER

AN ANTHONY BOURDAIN

TO MAILE,
SAWYER
& ELLERY

WD~50. Copyright © 2017 by Wylie Dufresne. All rights reserved. Printed in China. No part of this book may be used or reproduced in any manner whatsoever without written permission except in the case of brief quotations embodied in critical articles and reviews. For information address HarperCollins Publishers, 195 Broadway, New York, NY 10007.

HarperCollins books may be purchased for educational, business, or sales promotional use. For information please e-mail the Special Markets Department at SPsales@harper collins.com.

FIRST EDITION

Designed by Suet Yee Chong
Photography by Eric Medsker

Library of Congress Cataloging-in-Publication Data has been applied for.

ISBN 978-0-06-231853-4

17 18 19 20 21   ID/IM   10 9 8 7 6 5 4 3 2 1

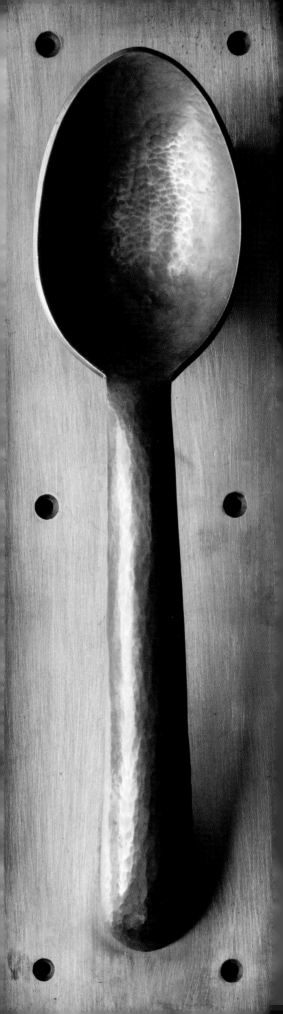

CONTENTS

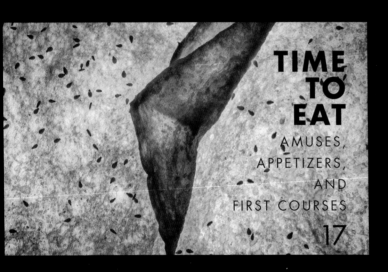

INTRODUCTION

TIMING IS EVERYTHING

This is my first cookbook, and I know what a lot of people are thinking: It's late. wd~50 opened in the spring of 2003 and closed eleven years later, on November 30, 2014. In theory, I could have written several books by now: one about my years at 71 Clinton Fresh Food, another about the early days at wd~50, maybe a cocktail book on the side. The truth is, I wasn't ready. For years I just didn't think I had enough to contribute to the dialogue. I have been amassing and devouring cookbooks since my early twenties—as a young cook I spent every spare penny on them—but I was always daunted by the idea of putting my own book on the shelf with the greats: Michel Bras's *Essential Cuisine,* Thomas Keller's *The French Laundry Cookbook,* Jean-Louis Palladin's *Cooking with the Seasons.* At last count, I had more than 1,200 cookbooks in my apartment and another thousand or so in storage, and my hope is that my own book will do for young, up-and-coming chefs what so many other cookbooks have done for me.

Sharing information and mentoring others is what wd~50 was all about. I wanted it to be a good restaurant, of course, but more than that, I wanted it to be a place where we were learning constantly. Early in my career I realized that chefs all over the city were cooking things in a certain way just because they were taught to do it that way. They knew how to sear a steak or make a sauce or poach an egg, but they didn't know why (or if) the method was the right one. Why does cream have to be whipped cold but milk only foams when it's hot? Why do you have to poach an egg in boiling water? Our approach at wd~50 was to ask those questions and a thousand others so we could understand exactly what was happening to our food at every step of the process.

Not long after wd~50 opened, our science-driven approach to cooking became a somewhat heated topic in the food world. A meal at wd~50 was different from anything anyone had experienced at a "fine dining" restaurant in New York, and not just because the tablecloths were missing. We were manipulating ingredients and pushing people to experience food in a whole new way. While some diners found that to be thrilling and exciting, others balked and said we were taking the soul out of cooking and behaving like mad scientists in the kitchen.

I can tell you this: We weren't making our food different for the sake of being different. We weren't saying, "Look what we can do!" We were saying, "Look what cooking can be." We were genuinely excited, and our goal was to bring that excitement to the plate. I used to tell the cooks, "I don't care if people say they don't like the flavors we put together, but I don't want anyone to ever say the food isn't well made." Everything we did, we did at the highest level, to the best of our abilities. And when people asked me what kind of food we served, I didn't call it "molecular gastronomy" or "modern cuisine" or "innovative cooking." I just said, "It's hot food that tastes good."

THE MENTORS

Alfred Portale, the chef at New York City's Gotham Bar and Grill, sat me down in 1993 and told me, in the nicest possible way, that I might not be cut out for kitchen work. Gotham was one of the city's most influential restaurants at the time, and I had no business working there. I was twenty-three, still in cooking school at the French Culinary Institute, and I was in way over my head. The only reason I got the job in the first place was that my cousin was Alfred's neighbor. Alfred was the high priest of architectural plating: His dishes were towering, gravity-defying showstoppers. One of the most popular ones was a seafood salad, and I just couldn't do it. You were supposed to put a pile of the seafood salad down the middle of the plate, affix a fan of avocado slices to the side as if they were scaling the seafood, then burrow a hole in the middle of the seafood and mount a spiraling plume of seven kinds of lettuce so they'd shoot up like a geyser.

I have fairly decent hand-eye coordination—and a deep appreciation for art and sculpture from my graphic-designer mother—but this salad just killed me. I'd manage to get the greens to spindle up and then they'd unbundle and the whole thing would fall apart. Guys who had been working for Alfred forever would come over, remake the thing in thirty seconds, and show me how to do it again and again. Alfred, who is a great friend and mentor to this day, saw me struggling for more than a year and finally suggested that I think long and hard about whether cooking was the right career path. I had to take a break for knee surgery at the time, and during the few months I was out of commission, I followed Alfred's advice. I thought long and hard, and I decided to double down and try for a job at one of the most intense restaurants in the city: Jean-Georges Vongerichten's JoJo.

I was reading Jean-Georges's *Simple Cuisine* at the time, and I was totally blown away by it. Here was a chef who was rooted in French cuisine but completely redefining it. He was taking stocks, creams, and butters out and replacing them with juices, flavored oils, and vinaigrettes. It was smart and exciting, and I wanted to be a part of it. Despite misspelling *Vongerichten* when I dropped off my résumé, Jean-Georges's team at JoJo let me trail for a day and, after that, I was dead-set on getting a job there. I called the chef de cuisine twice a day for several days in a row. I don't know if I broke his spirit or if he actually needed someone, but he gave in. I was assigned to the garde manger section.

On the day I started at JoJo, one of the cooks told me that in the past few months, twenty other people had taken the job and either quit or been fired. I never knew why, but I welcomed the challenge. At the time, Jean-Georges had only two restaurants: JoJo and Vong. Monday, Wednesday, and Friday he was at JoJo; Tuesday, Thursday, and Saturday he was at Vong. On Monday nights he expedited in the kitchen, and he was an arm's length away from me all night long. "Hurry up, Willy! Hurry up!" I was Willy from day one. (He still calls me Willy, and every person in Spain and France calls me Willy because of him.) During my time with him, Jean-Georges dished out some of the finest soul-crushing commentary in kitchen history:

- **"You make one, I make two!"** he would yell, demeaning my speed. I've used that line ever since.
- **"You're too slow for New York!"** For a foreign man with an impenetrably thick Alsatian accent to yell this at someone who grew up in New York is so embarrassing.
- **"Don't tell anyone you work here."** That's another one of my favorites. It's so great. And to a certain extent he was serious—he trained in the traditional French kitchen system, where the names on your résumé told the story of your character.

Watching Jean-Georges at the stove was the best training imaginable for a young chef. He'd come back to the line to cook for a VIP and we'd step aside and study his every move. He had a grace about him, an ability to make everything look effortless. And he was thinking differently from everyone else. He'd coat sweetbreads with chestnuts and then drizzle them with a truffle vinaigrette, sharp and acidic enough to keep the dish bright and alive despite all those rich, earthy elements. He sauced better than anyone. Juices and flavored oils were everywhere. I remember looking at a container of translucent bright red stuff and discovering it was lobster oil. At some point these techniques became commonplace in New York kitchens, but at the time, the things we were doing were crazy.

After almost three years at JoJo, I was tapped to help open Jean-Georges on Central Park, which was going to be the chef's flagship restaurant. I was the saucier, and over the next three years I learned how to butcher and make sauces, and how to manage other cooks when I was promoted to sous-chef. But more than that, I got a lifelong lesson in focus and restraint. The philosophy of Jean-Georges and Didier

(Text continues on page 12.)

(Text continues from page 3.)

Virot, the chef de cuisine, was "take away, take away." While other chefs were piling on sauces and garnishes, we were simplifying. Everything on the plate had to be perfect, because there was nowhere to hide. When Jean-Georges signed menus for diners, he used to write, "Keep it simple." That said it all.

I opened Prime, a Las Vegas steakhouse, for Jean-Georges in 1999, and near the end of my stint there, Sam Mason, then the pastry chef for Jean-Louis Palladin, told me that Jean-Louis was looking for a sous-chef to open a restaurant in New York. I jumped at the chance: It was like going to work for Obi-Wan Kenobi. I was on the opening team, but I left after just five months. For years, I never told anyone I worked for Jean-Louis, because I didn't even come close to the requisite one-year minimum. I still regret that I didn't get to have much time with him, but my dad had asked me if I'd help open a place on Clinton Street that had investors but no chef. It was going to be called 71 Clinton Fresh Food.

CLINTON STREET

When I started serving my own food for the first time, at 71 Clinton, the menu surprised everyone. Jim Nelson wrote about the restaurant's effect on the Lower East Side for the *New York Times* a few years after we opened:

> These were dishes the Lower East Side had never seen: edamame-and-rye-bread-crusted sea bass, duck with a bok-choy-and-confit baton. And though most of the people who lived in the neighborhood could not afford $20 entrees, the prices were markedly lower than those of uptown restaurants. The critics swooned, and soon the house was packed every night with destination diners. They'd line up outside, hoping to nab one of the 30 seats, chattering on their cellphones and hanging out near the bodega next door, looking at first a little lost and scared. Witnessing the scene at 71 Clinton—the line of cars; the willingness of people to "go slumming" in the Lower East Side—others swung into action. Within months, local real-estate agents were sending out commercial flyers advertising available spaces in the neighborhood and encouraging new businesses to piggyback on the success of 71 Clinton.

Despite all the great press we got at the restaurant, one key detail was consistently misunderstood: I never owned the place. People would say, "Have you been to Wylie Dufresne's restaurant?" I kept saying, "It's not mine, I'm just the chef."

But few people heard me, so almost everyone was confused when, just two years into 71 Clinton and with heaps of positive reviews, I announced that I was leaving to open a restaurant across the street. I wanted to grow, and that wasn't possible at 71, where the kitchen was big enough for only three cooks and where I had to cook by the house rules. The menu always had to include a salad, a pasta, and a vegetarian entrée. Across the street, I'd be able to make my own rules, and Jean-Georges made it happen: I went to meet him at 9:30 one morning to tell him I wanted to open my own place and that I had no idea how to do it. He said he'd help me, and just like that, he and his partner, Phil Suarez, became my business partners.

I wanted to do fine dining in a different way, a Lower East Side way. My father understood what I was thinking. We're both a little left-of-center: We like messing with the status quo, and we realized that while we loved dining in all the great restaurants uptown, we really weren't of that world.

THE END

The life of wd~50 is a New York story, from the very beginning—when we took over an old bodega on Clinton Street in 2002—to the last dinner we served, in November 2014. Changing the face of the city's Lower East Side was ultimately the very thing that killed us: Real-estate developers razed the building to make way for luxury condominiums. What's more New York than that? We could have camped out for the last few years of our lease, but we would have been in the middle of a construction pit, in a tense relationship with the landlord. We had no choice but to tell everyone we were closing and spend the next six months cooking our hearts out.

I miss the restaurant and the people there like crazy. I think I'd still be able to walk those 5,000 square feet with my eyes closed. I haven't been back to that stretch of Clinton Street since our final night. I can't. But when I realized that wd~50's days were numbered, I became singularly focused on documenting everything we had done there, from the first night of service until the last. I wanted to remember it all—every crazy idea, every surprising discovery, every mistake, everything. This book is a window into our world. As much as I miss wd~50, I find some peace in what we're leaving behind: discoveries that have helped inform cooking around the world, and techniques that could become part of the conversation for years to come. On the following pages, you'll meet the amazing cast of characters who made it all happen, and you'll see how our obsession with research and experimentation led to some very exciting food. I hope you get out of this what all of us at wd~50 got out of our time there: We became better cooks, we became smarter, and we had a hell of a lot of fun along the way.

FROM POPS

Wylie and I worked together our whole lives. As a kid, Wylie would work with me at summer jobs, sometimes peeling potatoes at the Olympia Tea Room in Little Compton.

I brought him in to 71 Clinton Fresh Foods, and largely because of his cooking, 71 gained tremendous notoriety. It was cool because it was a little place with food that maybe two- and three-star places uptown weren't serving. Wylie was inventive, but within the parameters of convention. He was executing great technique and putting great flavors together. I always saw it as being like an ambitious restaurant in a far-flung arrondissement of Paris.

Abstract artists start out grounded and with a solid experience of format, and then their minds take them on a journey. That's what wd~50 was about. Wylie had gone from a traditional jazz musician to an avant-garde jazz musician. And they didn't want that. It's like when Dylan went electric at the Newport Folk Festival— I was there! I was so excited because it was so good.

I saw Wylie's food and my idea of design as parallel universes; I wanted the design to reflect the food and what the food said. There were never tablecloths. It was meant to be a place where people could go dressed like normal working guys and gals, and, in my fantasy, people in tuxedos two tables away could also be comfortable.

One of the reasons we never had a power wine list was to highlight the interesting, natural, well-thought-out wines being produced by young people, by new people, with new intentions.

You know, I didn't expect everybody to like it. I don't know if I expected anyone to like it. But I expected a response. That's all I wanted. Not "It's good enough." Or "It's in the safe zone." Criticism is valid. No response is not.

We didn't try to be different for difference's sake. We did what we thought was interesting and what was fun. And we asked ourselves questions about how and why things always were the way they were in restaurants, and then we set out to find our own answers to those questions.

—Dewey, aka Dad

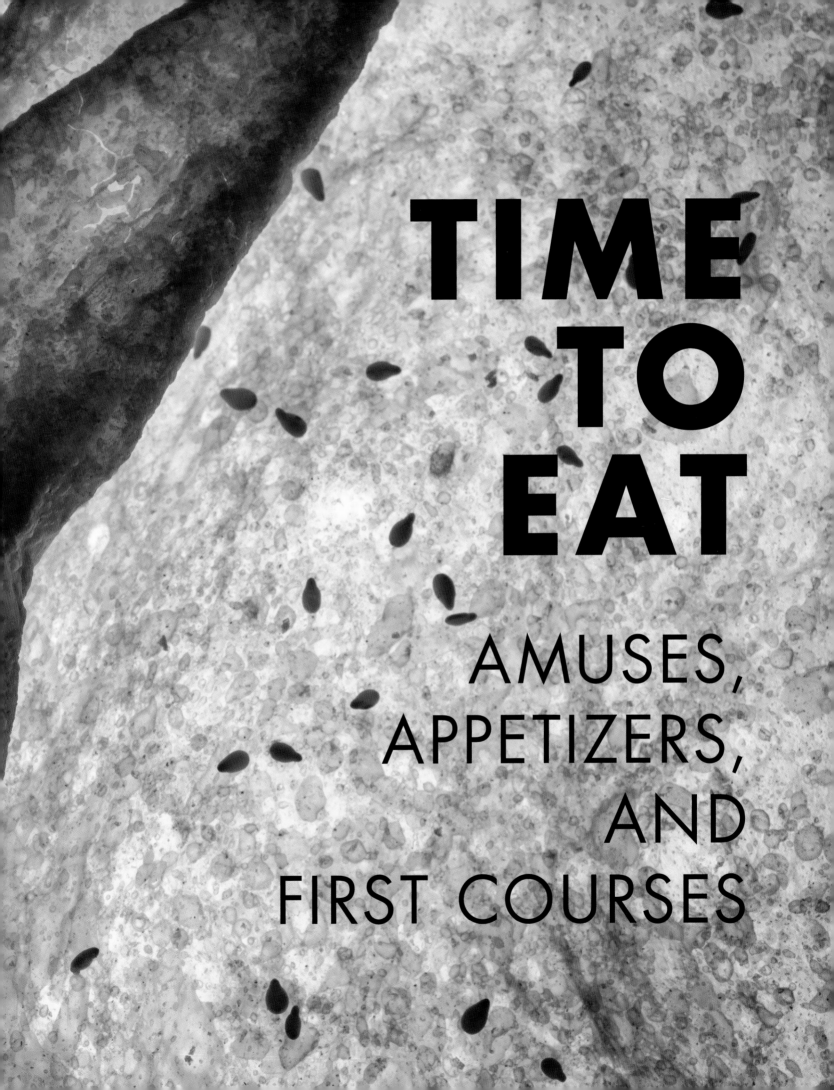

TIME
TO
EAT

AMUSES,
APPETIZERS,
AND
FIRST COURSES

LAVASH
THE FIRST BITE

I've always appreciated the circus of bread service at fancy restaurants. *"Sir, your tiny loaf of just-baked bread has been in front of you for six minutes so it's certainly cold! Let us bring you a new one, warm!"* I have to remember not to eat four rolls and ruin my appetite for dinner.

We didn't serve bread at wd~50, and that will seem odd to anyone who knows how much I love it. But when I'm at places like Jean-Georges or Mugaritz or Noma, I can't help myself—I eat too much of it—and we didn't want to create that conundrum at wd~50. We didn't want someone like me to have a third roll and then skip dessert.

But we had to welcome people with something. Johnny Iuzzini, who was then the pastry chef at Jean-Georges, passed along a recipe for lavash—a Middle Eastern flatbread—to our pastry chef, Sam Mason. Sam got it extra-thin and crackly and delicious, and we sprinkled sesame seeds on the first batch. It became the signature first bite of every wd~50 meal.

After "Can we have some more?," the question we heard most often was "How do you get it so thin?" The truth is that it was a bitch to make: Someone had to pull bread for four or five hours a day. At the end of wd~50's run, the one place in the restaurant with visible, obvious wear and tear was the floor in the pastry kitchen, broken down from the repetitive motion of nonstop lavash-making. We made it every day—or I should say the *stages* and younger cooks made it every day. Once he devised the recipe, Sam Mason made sure he never came to work early enough to do it. Christina Tosi, who worked under Sam, somehow found the Zen in the process. Alex Stupak, who took over as pastry chef in 2006, vowed that he wouldn't ever pull the bread. I'm pretty sure he kept his word.

Regardless of who made the lavash, we ended up with something that wasn't at all filling—but that had all the crunchy, flaky appeal of great bread.

SERVES 10 TO 15

535 grams water

25 grams fresh yeast

735 grams bread flour

5 grams sugar

15 grams salt, plus more as needed

Cooking spray

All-purpose flour

Whole milk

Sesame seeds

1. In a stand mixer fitted with the paddle attachment, combine the water and yeast and whisk to dissolve. Add the bread flour and mix on low speed until the dough becomes a mass, about 1 minute.

2. Turn off the mixer, add the sugar and salt, and mix on medium speed for about 10 minutes. The dough should be smooth and shiny and pull away from the sides of the bowl. Coat a large bowl with cooking spray, place the dough in the bowl, spray the top of the dough, and cover with plastic wrap. Proof in a warm spot until doubled in size, 2 to 3 hours.

3. Dust a flat surface and a bench knife with all-purpose flour. Divide the dough into portions weighing between 100 and 125 grams. Lightly shape the pieces into balls. Place the balls on a sheet pan, cover the pan loosely with plastic wrap, and proof at room temperature for 45 minutes. "Smack them down" with your knuckles and move to the refrigerator to proof for another 5 hours.

4. Gently flatten each portion with the back of your hand, dusting the balls with flour as you go. Shape each flattened portion into a small oval, like pizza dough: Move your hands along the edges, allowing the weight of the dough to pull itself down. Layer the portions between plastic wrap on a sheet pan and chill for 4 hours.

5. Heat the oven to 375°F.

6. Place some whole milk in a spray bottle. Coat a half-sheet pan with cooking spray and pull one portion of the dough over the corners, working in a clockwise manner. Spray the top of the dough with whole milk and sprinkle with salt and sesame seeds. Bake, rotating once, until golden brown, 7 to 10 minutes. Remove from the oven, break into shards, and serve. Repeat with the remaining portions of dough.

CORNED DUCK, RYE CRISPS, PURPLE MUSTARD, HORSERADISH CREAM

This was a snack that never got old to me. There were months—maybe years—when I ate at least one a day. As the years passed it was the only dish left from the original menu, the last man standing. I kept it on for that reason alone.

The inspiration and flavors of the dish are those of the Lower East Side: corned beef on rye with mustard and celery soda. My dad and I would go to Katz's Delicatessen when I was a kid, and that was always my order. To this day, one of my all-time favorite pairings on the planet is a corned beef sandwich and a Dr. Brown's Cel-Ray soda.

This dish told the story of who I was and where our restaurant was—it reflected our *terroir* as well as anything we ever created.

The following recipe is in quantities intended for a commerical kitchen. You can make smaller amounts of the duck and brine, but it is difficult to make smaller quantities of the other elements—they taste good on many different things and will keep well in the refrigerator.

SERVES 6 TO 8

Purple Mustard and Miso Sauce (page 24)

18 to 24 Rye Crisps (page 25)

18 to 24 slices Corned Duck (page 25)

12 to 24 slices Honey Garlic (page 26)

Horseradish Cream (page 26)

Baby celery sprouts

1. On each plate, place 3 dots of purple mustard about 1½ inches apart. Put 3 rye crisps on each dot and pipe the purple mustard in a thin layer on top of it.

2. Roll 3 slices of the corned duck into an oval that fits the rye crisp and place 1 on top of each crisp. Place 2 or 3 slices of honey garlic on top of the duck. Squirt a little horseradish cream on top of the duck and garlic.

3. Garnish with baby celery sprouts.

PURPLE MUSTARD
AND MISO SAUCE

I was introduced to purple mustard while I was working for Jean-Georges Vongerichten. It's Dijon mustard
mixed with lees left from pressing wine. He bought his
version, but we set out to make our own—with no access to red wine lees. This is our improvised method.
The result was fantastic and winey and as purple as we
could have hoped. We bumped up the umami of the
sauce with a touch of miso at the end.

2 sprigs thyme
3 black peppercorns, toasted
750 grams (1 bottle) red wine
1 head garlic, broken into cloves
5 shallots, sliced
115 grams Dijon mustard
15 grams red miso

1. Place the thyme and peppercorns in a sachet.
2. In a large saucepan, combine the wine, garlic, shallots, and sachet. Bring to a simmer over medium heat
   and reduce, uncovered, to a syrup, about 1 hour.
3. Remove the sachet and pass the syrup and solids through a tamis into a clean bowl. Whisk in the
   mustard and miso. Let cool and place in a squeeze
   bottle. Refrigerate until ready to use.

RYE CRISPS

The corned duck dish fostered our relationship with Moishe's, an orthodox Jewish bakery on Second Avenue where we bought the rye for the rye crisps. I tell you, we shopped there for ten straight years and we never failed to forget the Jewish holidays. You'd think we would have been smart enough to remember that Rosh Hasshanah was coming and that we should buy an extra ten loaves to put in the freezer. Nope. We would always forget and have to scramble to find another source.

I owe the technique for the rye crisps to my friend Josh Eden, a chef known as Shorty, who told me about an idea he had for putting a piece of bread through a pasta machine. We bought whole loaves of Moishe's rye, froze them solid, then sliced them lengthwise on the deli slicer and sent them through the pasta machine several times. Bread compressed like that is great, as every kid knows from taking a slice of white bread and squeezing it into a tiny ball.

1 loaf rye bread, with seeds
30 grams butter, melted
Maldon salt

1. Trim the crusts from the rye bread and place the loaf in the freezer.
2. Once frozen, thinly slice the loaf lengthwise—the opposite direction of how you'd cut it to make sandwiches—to yield 4 long slabs. Roll the slabs through a pasta machine on setting number 6. Save the remainder of the loaf for anything you'd like.
3. Brush the pressed bread with melted butter and sprinkle with Maldon salt.
4. Heat the oven to 200°F.
5. Cut the slabs into 2 x 1-inch rectangles and place on a sheet pan between two silicone baking mats. Toast in the oven just until dry and crispy, about 20 minutes—you don't want any color. Hold at room temperature until ready to use.

CORNED DUCK

Corning as a curing technique goes back centuries. You "corn" something by putting it in a brine or packing it in salt, and long ago salt was the size of corn kernels, hence the name. Although our reference point was corned beef, we wanted to reinterpret the dish, so we chose duck. It has delicious fat, just like beef. And we gave the corned duck the look of pastrami, because it's a better-looking deli meat; when you slice it, it has that nice dark edge of spices.

To achieve this look, we put a cast-iron pan on the flattop and got it so hot that everybody was terrified. Then we took the pan off the heat—it had to be off the heat, otherwise it would catch on fire—and we put the duck breast in the pan and pressed on it. The pan was so hot that smoke would billow out like crazy, and 30 seconds later there would be this jet-black burned crust. We cooled it and cut it paper-thin and it was beautiful, with a flavor and look that evoked a classic deli meat.

8 grams coriander seeds
5 grams mustard seeds
5 grams fennel seeds
1 cardamom pod
25 whole cloves
3 cinnamon sticks
2 grams black peppercorns
1 gram cumin seeds
1 gram pink peppercorns
3 cloves garlic
2 sprigs thyme
1 bay leaf
1 kilogram water
25 grams kosher salt
20 grams sugar
3.75 grams Instacure #1
2 Moulard duck breasts, about 375 to 400 grams each

1. In a dry pan, toast all of the spices over low heat until fragrant, about 1 minute. Set aside.
2. In a large stockpot, combine the toasted spices, garlic, thyme, bay leaf, water, salt, and sugar. Bring to a simmer, stirring until the salt and sugar dissolve. Let cool, then add the Instacure #1. Stir to combine.
3. Pour the brine into a clean container. Add the duck breasts fat side up and weight down with a plate or other heavy object so they stay submerged. Place in the refrigerator and brine for 72 hours.
4. After 3 days, remove the duck from the brine and pat dry.
5. Heat a large cast-iron pan over high heat until smoking. Pull the pan off the heat and place the duck in, fat side down. Return to the heat and sear, draining the rendered fat until the fat cap has blackened evenly and has rendered down to about a ¼-inch thickness, 2 to 4 minutes. Let cool.
6. Vacuum-seal the breasts in a cryovac bag and cook sous vide in a 136°F water bath for 2 hours. Cool in an ice bath.
7. When completely cool, slice the breasts on a deli slicer on setting #1, with the fat cap facing you. You want very thin slices.

HONEY GARLIC

50 cloves garlic
Kosher salt
Clover honey

1. Place the garlic in a large pot of salted water and bring to a boil over high heat. As soon as the water begins to boil, take the pot off the heat, remove the garlic, and shock in an ice bath.
2. Place the garlic cloves back in the water and place over high heat. Bring the water back to a boil. As soon as it begins to boil, take the pot off the heat, remove the garlic, and shock in an ice bath. Repeat 8 to 10 times until the garlic is just tender.
3. Place the garlic in a large plastic container and cover with clover honey. Close the container, wrap in plastic, and let sit at room temperature for 2 months. Move the container to the refrigerator and let sit for 1 more month before using.

HORSERADISH CREAM

Horseradish was not one of my sandwich flavor memories from childhood, but when Fran Derby, part of our opening team, suggested adding it to the dish, I couldn't argue with him. Duck and horseradish are old friends.

60 grams fresh horseradish
35 grams water
35 grams grapeseed oil
115 grams cream cheese
1 lemon, juiced
Kosher salt
Freshly ground black pepper

Blend all of the ingredients until smooth. Place in a squeeze bottle and refrigerate until ready to use.

PICKLED BEEF TONGUE, FRIED MAYONNAISE, ONION STREUSEL

The story of fried mayonnaise starts at a dinner party at my brother-in-law Dave Arnold's house, where I overheard someone say, "Wouldn't it be cool if you could deep-fry mayonnaise?"

I don't even really like mayonnaise, but a light went on, and I imagined that if I could figure it out, McDonald's would want to buy my idea and I'd get to retire early.

Once we had deep-fried mayonnaise, we needed to build a dish around it. We landed on an appetizer inspired by a roast beef sandwich: beef tongue, lettuce, tomato, and mayonnaise. It was a tip of the hat to my old man, who once owned a sandwich shop in Providence, Rhode Island. The beef tongue was a beloved fixture on the wd~50 menu in the early years, and it got a second life when we reconfigured the garnishes into a hot dog topping for the cocktail bar PDT.

SERVES 4

30 grams Tomato Molasses (page 30)
12 slices Pickled Beef Tongue (page 30)
Olive oil
Balinese salt crystals

10 grams Red Onion Streusel (page 31)
2 leaves romaine, green parts cut into 12 small triangles, ribs brunoised
8 cubes Fried Mayonnaise (page 31)

1. With a small offset spatula, sauce each plate with about 1½ teaspoons of tomato molasses on the left side in a counter-clockwise motion.

2. Place 3 slices of tongue to the right of the tomato molasses and dress with a few drops of olive oil and a few Balinese salt crystals.

3. Arrange a vertical line of red onion streusel and brunoise of romaine ribs to the far right of the tongue. Place the fried mayo next to the tongue. Arrange 3 romaine triangles along the length of the tongue.

TOMATO MOLASSES

400 grams tomatoes

100 grams butter

100 grams molasses

Kosher salt

Tabasco sauce

1. In a pot of hard-boiling water, blanch the tomatoes for 30 seconds. Shock in ice water. Peel and seed the tomatoes, then roughly chop.
2. In a saucepan, combine the butter and molasses and melt over low heat. Add the tomatoes and cook over very, very, very low heat until the mixture thickens and takes on the unctuous texture of tomato paste, 6 to 8 hours. Let cool.
3. Blend the mixture to a smooth paste, then season with a pinch of salt and Tabasco. Think ketchup: sweet, savory, with a hint of tang. Refrigerate until ready to use.

PICKLED BEEF TONGUE

2 calf tongues (about 1 kilogram each)

2 kilograms Standard Brine (recipe follows)

15 grams butter

60 grams diced celery (about ½ inch)

60 grams diced onion (about ½ inch)

60 grams diced carrot (about ½ inch)

2 cloves garlic

15 grams grated fresh ginger

5 allspice berries

90 grams brown sugar

240 grams rice vinegar

2.25 kilograms chicken stock or water

47 grams kosher salt

1. Soak the tongues in cold water for 1 day, changing the water once.
2. Fill an injector needle with brine and inject each tongue at its tip, base, and middle. Submerge the tongues in the remainder of the brine. Refrigerate for 1 week.
3. In a large stockpot, melt the butter over medium heat. Add the celery, onion, carrot, and garlic and cook for 5 minutes. Add the ginger, allspice, brown sugar, rice vinegar, chicken stock, and salt and bring to a simmer. Add the tongues and cook over very low heat until tender, 2 to 3 hours.
4. Allow the tongues to cool until able to handle. Wearing gloves, slide your fingers under the skin of each tongue and gently peel it away. (If the tongue is braised properly, this should be easy to do.)
5. Strain the braising liquid into a clean container and place the tongues back in. Let cool.
6. Trim the muscle on the underside of each tongue. Slice the tongues lengthwise on a deli slicer on setting #0.5. For clean slices, it's useful to par-freeze the tongues, but do not freeze them entirely, as it will compromise the flavor and texture of the meat.

STANDARD BRINE

25 grams kosher salt

20 grams sugar

3 grams Instacure #1

1 kilogram water

In a large saucepan, combine all of the ingredients and stir over high heat until the sugar and salts dissolve. Let cool.

RED ONION STREUSEL

1 red onion, diced
60 grams all-purpose flour
100 grams almond flour
5 grams kosher salt
120 grams butter, melted

1. Set the oven or dehydrator to 160°F.
2. Spread the onion on a sheet pan and bake/dehydrate until dry, about 12 hours. Let cool, then grind into a powder. Measure out 70 grams red onion powder (reserve the rest for another use).
3. Sift the red onion powder, all-purpose flour, almond flour, and salt into a large bowl. Mix in the butter until combined. Pack the dough firmly into a shallow metal pan and freeze.
4. Heat the oven to 200°F.
5. Line a half-sheet pan with parchment. Using the fine holes on a box grater, grate the frozen streusel onto the pan. Bake for 10 minutes. Pull off a spoonful and cool it quickly on a countertop. The streusel should be crunchy-chewy without the raw flavor of red onion. Hold at room temperature until ready to use.

FRIED MAYONNAISE

This produces more than four servings. You can freeze extra breaded mayo cubes on a tray and keep them for when your next fried mayo urge strikes.

3 grams low-acyl gellan gum
250 grams cold whole milk
500 grams grapeseed oil
5 grams silver sheet gelatin
30 grams Dijon mustard
30 grams lemon juice
12 grams kosher salt
1 gram freshly ground black pepper

1 egg
1 egg yolk
50 grams all-purpose flour
60 grams panko breadcrumbs, finely ground
Neutral oil, for deep-frying

1. In a blender, shear the gellan into the cold milk. Pour the mixture into a saucepan.
2. Bring the mixture to a boil over high heat and cook, whisking constantly, until the gellan is fully hydrated. You will be able to tell from the texture of the mixture: When gellan gum is heated, it swells rapidly around 122°F to form a thick, pasty suspension. With continued heating the suspension loses viscosity around 194°F, signifying complete hydration.
3. Heat the grapeseed oil to 210°F in a small saucepan.
4. Dissolve the gelatin in the hot milk mixture, then slowly whisk in the hot oil, being careful to add only a little at a time so you don't break the emulsion.
5. In a separate saucepan, gently warm the mustard, lemon juice, salt, and pepper. Fold into the hot milk mixture. Transfer the mixture to a container in which you can comfortably use an immersion blender and blend the mixture as it cools—it should be just slightly warm to the touch and completely fluid before you spread it onto a plastic-lined half-sheet pan. Lay plastic over the top of the mayonnaise and smooth the surface with a plastic bench scraper. Let cool.
6. In a wide flat bowl, whisk together the whole egg and egg yolk. Place the flour and panko in separate bowls.
7. Cut the set mayonnaise gel into 1-inch cubes. Coat each cube with the flour, then the egg wash, then the panko. Refrigerate in a single layer on a sheet pan under plastic wrap until serving.
8. Right before serving, deep-fry the mayonnaise cubes (see page 32) at 375°F for 2 to 3 minutes, just until golden brown outside and creamy within, then warm the fried mayonnaise cubes in a 200°F oven for 2 to 3 minutes. Serve warm!

HOW TO
DEEP-FRY MAYONNAISE

When I set out to make deep-fried mayonnaise, I figured I just needed to firm it up so I could cut it into cubes, bread it, and fry it. Gelatin seemed like the obvious solution. I dissolved gelatin in a tiny amount of water and blended it into a traditional mayonnaise. But when I put the breaded cubes into the fryer, all hell broke loose. Water and hot oil do not like each other. Freezing didn't work either. The answer eventually came from Chris Young, a research chef at the Fat Duck who later became the chef behind *Modernist Cuisine* and the website ChefSteps. He suggested incorporating gellan, a gelling agent with a high heat tolerance, into our mayonnaise.

At the time, we were really starting to understand gums and the science behind them, thanks in part to a great book called *Handbook of Hydrocolloids*. We figured out that to make deep-fried mayo, we would need both gelatin (to firm it up for portioning) *and* gellan (to keep it stable in the fryer). But as we continued experimenting, we hit another hurdle: The eggs kept curdling in the fryer. So we added milk, which gave us a water-based element needed to hydrate the gellan and help it do its magic. We blended the gellan into the milk, brought it up to a boil, added bloomed gelatin, and then started beating in the oil. As the temperature in the pot dropped, the gellan started setting and the whole mixture broke. I was trying to mount oil into a gel—a liquid into a solid. That was when I had the aha moment: I needed to keep everything above a certain temperature so the gellan and the gelatin were both in the same state: liquid, not solid. Gellan sets, or forms its gel matrix, very quickly when it drops below 180°F. I had to keep the oil hot.

This should have been the moment of truth, but when the mixture set up and we cut it into cubes, it was a warm, solid gel. It wasn't creamy. We didn't want to fry a solid gel, we wanted to fry a fluid gel—we needed a little motion. So this time, when our mayonnaise started to set, we used an immersion blender to purée it into a "fluid gel." By doing this, we successfully decimated the gellan's matrix. When we chilled the mixture, our old friend gelatin came to the party and firmed up the mayonnaise so we could cut it into cubes. We then breaded it, fried it briefly for color, and popped it in the oven for a minute to heat it through and effectively melt the gelatin once again. We cut open the cubes and voilà!—deep-fried mayonnaise.

EVERYTHING BAGEL, TROUT THREADS, CRISPY CREAM CHEESE

I love a dish where everything is not what it seems. You see this and think, *Oh, a cute little bagel,* and then, upon eating it, you find out that it's a bagel made of ice cream. And who doesn't want to eat ice cream before dinner? It's a dish that invariably made people smile. Bagels are typically chewy, toasted, and crunchy; here they're creamy. Cream cheese is usually creamy; here it's crispy.

This is also a great example of how an idea works its way around the room—and how that process is the most effective way to bring a lot of expertise and perspective to one plate. The "everything bagel" ice cream was Sam Henderson's idea. She bought a bunch of bagels, toasted them, and infused them into a neutral crème anglais. Meanwhile, we had two pet projects going on, both of which made sense with the "everything bagel" theme: One was "salmon threads," trout threads here, which could stand in for lox; the other was a crisp cream cheese paper (we were constantly turning things into papers). Alex Stupak, our pastry chef at the time, had the great idea to put the ice cream in little savarin molds so it would look like a bagel. We rolled the ice cream bagels in everything-bagel spices, then we threw in some lightly pickled pearl onions to echo the onions a New Yorker would expect on a bagel with lox. We included a couple leaves of sorrel as a nice sour punch.

The dish got a lot of ink at the time—it went viral in the form that things went viral back then. But what I loved most about it (other than how it tasted) was that it was a real team effort.

SERVES 8

50 grams Trout Threads (page 36)

Pickled Pearl Onions (page 36)

8 Everything Bagels (page 37)

3 grams poppy seeds

6 grams white sesame seeds, toasted

8 wood sorrel leaves

8 shards Crispy Cream Cheese (page 37)

On each plate, place a raised semicircle of trout threads and place a small pile of pickled pearl onions next to it. On a work surface, sprinkle a "bagel" with poppy seeds and sesame seeds, then place it on top of the trout. Garnish with wood sorrel leaves and shards of cream cheese.

TROUT THREADS

Trout threads are the aquatic equivalent of *pork foo,* that Taiwanese/Chinese meat that is cooked and pushed and pulled and slowly dried over gentle heat until it becomes light and flossy.

I found this technique in a Japanese cookbook, where it was identified as a way of making fish furikake. The cooks dreaded making this stuff. You had to stand over it for *hours.* (This recipe can be accomplished in about 1 hour, but we made vast quantities at the restaurant.) You really had to be on it because the more you worked it, the fluffier it got. I told the cooks it was right when it looked like "fish hair" or pink insulation. It's a delicious condiment on almost anything—and well worth the effort.

> 25 grams kosher salt
>
> 25 grams sugar
>
> 450 grams skinless fillet of ocean trout
>
> 2 kilograms water
>
> 45 grams kombu
>
> Soy sauce
>
> Mirin
>
> 200 grams wood chips

1. In a small bowl, combine the salt and sugar. Coat the fish liberally on both sides and let sit for 2 hours. Rinse and pat dry.
2. In a pot, combine the water and kombu. Heat to 170°F and cook for 35 minutes. Discard the kombu and add the fish to the pot. Cook until the fish is cooked through, 8 to 10 minutes.
3. Remove the fish from the water and pat dry. Use your fingers to break the fish into small pieces roughly the size of prunes.
4. In a medium rondeau, heat a few scant drops of soy sauce and mirin over medium heat. Add the fish and start stirring and "fluffing" with a balloon whisk or flat wooden spatula. Continue stirring until the trout becomes dry, light, and threadlike, 1 to 2 hours. Remove from the heat and let cool.
5. Lay the trout threads in a quarter-sheet pan in a single shallow layer and place the pan in a smoker. Fill another quarter-sheet pan with ice and place on the rack below the trout. Ignite the wood chips and smoke the trout for 1 to 2 hours, or until the wood chips have expired; the inside shouldn't be hotter than 100° to 120°F. Hold the smoked trout threads in sealed containers at room temperature until ready to use.

PICKLED PEARL ONIONS

I love the texture of vacuum-made pickles, and you can eat them immediately after they come out of the vacuum chamber. But you can also make these pickles the old-fashioned way by combining the first three ingredients, bringing them to a boil, and pouring that over the onions.

> 20 grams red wine vinegar
>
> 40 grams water
>
> 20 grams sugar
>
> 5 red pearl onions, peeled and sliced into rounds

1. In a small saucepan, warm the vinegar and water over low heat. Add the sugar and stir until dissolved. Let cool.
2. Vacuum-seal the onions and pickling liquid in a cryovac bag. Refrigerate until ready to use.

EVERYTHING BAGEL

5 egg yolks

50 grams sugar

10 grams glucose powder

100 grams heavy cream

400 grams Bagel Milk (recipe follows)

0.2 gram guar gum

Caramel color

1. In a stand mixer, cream the yolks, sugar, and glucose until ribbons form.
2. In a medium saucepan, bring the cream and bagel milk to a gentle boil over medium-high heat. Place the yolk-sugar mixture in a metal bowl anchored by a wet towel. Using a whisk, slowly temper the yolk-sugar mixture with the hot dairy, adding it in a steady stream. Place over a double boiler and cook to about 160°F, whisking constantly. Strain through a chinois into a bowl and cool the mixture over an ice bath.
3. Pour the cooled mixture into a blender and blend in the guar gum until smooth.
4. Churn the mixture in an ice cream maker according to the manufacturer's instructions. Transfer the ice cream into a pastry bag and pipe into mini savarin molds. Freeze until solid.
5. Once frozen, turn the bagels out and spray with caramel color with an airbrush to resemble a lightly toasted bagel. Freeze until ready to use.

BAGEL MILK

975 grams whole milk

2 everything bagels, hard-toasted and crushed

In a medium saucepan, warm the milk over medium heat to a gentle simmer, then remove from the heat. Add the bagels and steep for 1 hour 30 minutes. Strain. This should yield about 400 grams of bagel milk.

CRISPY CREAM CHEESE

There's a lot of fat in cream cheese, and because fat doesn't dry, the solids in cream cheese need something to dry onto, a "substrate" in technical parlance. When we mixed methylcellulose with the cream cheese and dried it overnight, it came out shiny and crunchy and wonderful.

100 grams water

6 grams Methocel A4M methylcellulose

1.5 grams kosher salt

200 grams cream cheese

1. Bring the water to a boil, transfer to a blender, and shear in the methylcellulose and salt. Add the cream cheese to the blender and blend again. Cool to 50°F.
2. Spread the mixture onto sheets of acetate and dehydrate at 155°F overnight.
3. Break the mixture into irregular shards. Store in an airtight container at room temperature until ready to use.

BLOODLESS SAUSAGE, SMOKED ALMONDS, LILY BULBS, MUSHROOM

We had a constant need for vegetarian options on our tasting menu. When we set out to make vegetarian sausage, our sous-chef, Reggie Soang, started working with Forbidden rice and beet juice, trying to get something that would look and taste meaty. I thought we should call it "bloodless sausage" because, at the very least, we could have a little fun with the vegetarians.

Reggie's flavors were there early on, but it took some time to get the texture right. The addition of masa (the alkalized corn dough used to make tortillas) helped. Sausage also requires a lot of fat, and unfortunately, pork fat is not widely considered to be vegetarian. So Reggie settled on coconut fat: It's solid at room temperature and mimics the properties of animal fat. The results were unimpeachable: It was damn good blood sausage, bloodless or not.

SERVES 8

8 Bloodless Sausages (page 40)

30 grams clarified butter

Smoked Marcona Almond Sauce
  (page 40)

Mushroom Jus (page 41)

Pickled Lily Bulbs (page 41)

Upland cress

1. Remove the sausages from their plastic-wrap straitjackets and place on a sheet pan. Warm in a CVap oven at 130° to 140°F for 8 minutes or in a regular oven at 250°F for 7 minutes.

2. Heat the clarified butter on a plancha or in a cast-iron pan over high heat. Sear the sausage links until browned on all sides. (If you're using a cast-iron pan, do this in batches, being sure not to crowd the pan.) Halve lengthwise.

3. Sauce each plate with smoked almond sauce and place a sausage on top. Sauce the bloodless link with mushroom jus, being careful not to let the jus and the almond sauce "commingle." Place 5 or 6 pieces of lily bulb on the side of the sausage and garnish with upland cress.

BLOODLESS SAUSAGES

Olive oil

65 grams onions, diced

50 grams coconut oil

125 grams masa

225 grams beet juice

50 grams Mushroom Jus (page 41)

100 grams Forbidden rice, cooked

100 grams farro, cooked (liquid reserved for Smoked
   Marcona Almond Sauce, right)

1 gram ground allspice

1 gram ground mace

5 grams kosher salt

1. In a medium saucepan, heat a slick of olive oil over medium heat. Add the onions and sweat until soft, about 10 minutes.
2. In a stand mixer fitted with the paddle attachment, beat the coconut oil into the masa until combined. With the mixer running, slowly add the beet juice.
3. Turn off the mixer and add the mushroom jus, rice, farro, onions, allspice, mace, and salt. Paddle at full speed until the mixture is homogenous.
4. Pull a sheet of plastic wrap tightly over your countertop so it adheres to the surface. Place the "farce" in a pastry bag and cut an opening about 1 inch in diameter. Pipe onto the plastic in a straight line, leaving about 1½ inches on either end for tying.
5. Roll tightly into a long cylinder (as you would a torchon), using a ruler or other straightedge to help keep the sausage perfectly straight. Torque the plastic wrap tightly around the farce and tie off at the ends. Pierce several times with a cake tester to remove air. Using butcher's twine, tie off the long cylinder into individual links about 2.5 inches long.
6. To cook: Set up a steamer. Place the links in a perforated pan over another pan of boiling water and cover with a lid or foil. Steam for 20 minutes.

To check for doneness, cut one link and give it a taste—it should remind you faintly of a tamale. If so, take the pan off the heat and let cool. If it tastes of raw masa, return to the steamer for 5 more minutes and check again. Refrigerate until ready to use.

SMOKED MARCONA ALMOND SAUCE

200 grams farro cooking liquid (reserved from
   Bloodless Sausages, left)

Smoked Marcona Almonds (recipe follows)

260 grams water

30 grams almond oil

2 grams kosher salt, plus more to taste

In a blender, process all the ingredients on high speed for at least 3 minutes. Taste and season with salt if needed. Pass through a fine tamis.

SMOKED MARCONA ALMONDS

140 grams Marcona almonds

200 grams wood chips

Place the almonds on a half-sheet pan inside of a smoker. Fill another half-sheet pan with ice and place it on the rack below the almonds. Ignite the wood chips and smoke the almonds until the chips expire or the almonds are sufficiently smoky. Hold at room temperature until ready to use.

MUSHROOM JUS

Olive oil

2 small red onions, sliced

1.5 quarts dried porcini mushrooms, soaked overnight and drained, liquid reserved

5 grams thyme leaves

1 bay leaf

1 head garlic, halved through the equator

1 quart cooked chickpeas

1. In a large stockpot, heat a slick of olive oil over medium heat. Sweat the onions and soaked mushrooms until lightly browned, about 10 minutes.
2. Add the thyme, bay leaf, and garlic and cook until fragrant, 2 to 3 minutes.
3. Measure out your mushroom soaking liquid and add one-third of that volume of water. Add to the pot with the chickpeas and bring to a boil. Reduce to a simmer, cover, and cook for 1½ hours. Strain. Reserve the chickpeas for another use.
4. Reduce the stock by two-thirds and check for consistency. The finished jus should be thick but not gluey.

PICKLED LILY BULBS

1 lily bulb, broken into petals and rinsed

225 grams Champagne vinegar

35 grams verjus reduction (verjus reduced by half its volume)

40 grams soy sauce

5 grams sugar

55 grams shallots, thinly sliced

7 grams fresh tarragon

Place the lily bulb petals in a heatproof container or large bowl. In a medium saucepan, combine the vinegar, verjus reduction, soy sauce, sugar, shallots, and tarragon. Bring to a boil over high heat. Pour the mixture over the lily bulbs and refrigerate overnight. Refrigerate until ready to use.

One of the plates that blew me away early on—and inspired our approach to plating at wd~50—was Jean-Georges's carrot soup. He built an unbelievable basket out of the thinnest pieces of carrot and filled it with tiny spheres of poached carrot, then placed that in the soup. I wouldn't say I ripped it off at 71 Clinton Street, but I borrowed it for a parsley root soup with crab salad served in a basket of thinly julienned celery root. My mom always said that it looked like a windswept beach: The color of the soup was a lot like sand, and the basket was like a classic Cape Cod fence buried in it.

My parents taught me to think visually. My mom is an artist in every sense of the word. She was trained in graphic design and for years owned a store called the Tin Woodsman that was filled with knickknacks and every funky cool thing you could imagine. Now she's a rare book dealer who brings old finds back to life. (Remember when your parents wrapped your school textbooks in a brown paper bag? My books were art objects when she was done with them.) My dad has his own, equally strong sense of style. When I was a kid he would bring home old neon clocks like they were lost puppies. He'd find them all beat up (this was when all the original neon dealers were going out of business) and he'd strip and paint them, then have a guy blow new neon for him in different colors. My parents always had unusual stuff in the kitchen, and they taught me that tableware can be as fun and playful as you want it to be. While my friends were eating dinner on functional white plates, I was having mine on radioactive-orange Fiestaware.

Growing up in the city also influenced my plating style in a huge way. Everywhere I looked I saw squares, rectangles, tubes, towers. New York has a lot of hard angles, but then there's a tree growing here, a fire escape casting a shadow there. That urban geometry informed so many of our dishes. It took me more than a decade to realize this, but soon after we opened, you could look at a plate and know it was from wd~50—and that the restaurant wasn't in the countryside or on the seashore: It was in New York City.

HAMACHI, MORCILLA, BABY TURNIP

This dish was not what it appeared to be—and I loved that about it. When you saw the plate, you figured it was a piece of hamachi nigiri, but we replaced the rice with tartare, so you were actually eating hamachi over hamachi. We finely chopped the more fibrous parts of the fillet for the tartare, and we sliced the luxurious, perfect midfillet piece to drape over the "rice." Then we torched it just the right amount to present the full range of hamachi's flavors and textures. On top we put a little micro shiso, taking our cue from Japanese chefs who often grate *sudachi* or yuzu right onto sushi.

For the plate, we sliced raw turnips very thinly, cryovac-compressed them in bright-yellow turnipseed oil, and shaped them into little cones. To add a savory, low note to the dish, we made a sauce of morcilla. Combining the rich, meaty sauce with lean fish and bitter turnips was a nice way to get bitter, sweet, salty, sour, and umami on a plate together. The swirl of the sauce was the work of Reggie Soang, and it was perfect. Every time I see it, I think of Saturday morning cartoons and the Tasmanian Devil whirling by.

SERVES 6

Hamachi midfillet (see Note, page 48), frozen solid

18 slices Baby Turnip (page 50)

Morcilla Sauce (page 51)

Hamachi Tartare (page 50)

Shiso

1. Shave the hamachi midfillet on a deli slicer on setting #2.

2. Stack 3 turnip slices and make an incision the length of the radius into the stack. Pull the sides of each slice toward one another to form a cone shape. There should be 3 cones per plate.

3. Warm the morcilla sauce and place in a squeeze bottle.

4. Sauce each plate by moving the tip of the squeeze bottle in a staggered orbit. When you are finished you should have an image that resembles a broad coil, or a Slinky.

5. On a separate plate, quenelle the tartare and place a piece of shaved hamachi on top. Brûlé with a blowtorch and transfer to on top of the morcilla sauce. Garnish with shiso.

HAMACHI

Hamachi is a wonderful fish to fillet. One of the things you'll notice is how the loin changes from end to end. For this dish, we broke each fillet into four sections. The parts by the head and tail are a bit fibrous, so we finely chopped those into a tartare that was almost like a paste; we diced the portion right above the tail to make a coarser tartare that we mixed with the paste; we froze the last piece (center cut) to slice on a deli slicer and drape over the tartare.

To create textural contrast, we hit those slices with a blowtorch for a few seconds. This changed the texture of the fish, because when you bite into the slice, you have cooked fish on top and raw fish underneath. But more important, by warming those oils in the fish, you bring out a completely different flavor profile. This was something I learned from Jean-Georges: When we cooked salmon, he would talk about gently cooking the fish, because oily fish can become overly fishy-tasting when you get it too hot. Cook it gently, and those oils warm up and the flavor changes in great ways.

Note: To prepare the hamachi for tartare, follow these steps:

1. Remove the collar, skin, and blood line.
2. Separate the side into two loins: top and bottom.
3. From the top loin, cut one portion of fish about 3 inches long (this should be the top 3 inches of fish, closest to the collar). Place this piece of fish in the freezer for a few hours, or until frozen solid.
4. Discard the tail meat and split each loin 50/50 by weight. Half should be used for "paste" and half should be used for a small dice. The midsection of the loins lend themselves to dicing; the outlying flesh lends itself to paste.
5. To make the paste, chop the flesh with a cleaver, dragging the meat against the cutting board to achieve a very smooth texture. Cut the remaining flesh into a small dice. Mix the dice and paste: This is the mix that will be seasoned into a tartare.

HAMACHI TARTARE

500 grams hamachi paste (see Note, page 48)
9 grams minced Preserved Lemon (recipe follows)
2 grams minced Shallot Confit (recipe follows)
2 grams kosher salt
1 gram minced green shiso

Mix all the ingredients and chill until ready to serve.

PRESERVED LEMON

6 lemons
100 grams kosher salt, plus more as needed
75 grams lemon juice

Quarter the lemons. Make a crosswise incision into the flesh, all the way down to the peel of the lemon. Layer the lemons in an airtight, sealable container with generous amounts of salt between each layer (100 grams is a guideline, but additional salt will not hurt the end product). Press down firmly but carefully on the lemons. Cover with the lemon juice. Layer with plastic. Close tightly and store in a dry area at room temperature for 90 days (these are ready and usable after 30 days, but letting them age longer makes for an even better preserved lemon). When ready to use, rinse and remove the flesh from the peel. Discard the flesh—the peel is the thing you're after here.

SHALLOT CONFIT

5 large shallots, brunoised
Grapeseed oil

Place the shallots in a small pot and cover with oil. Cook on very low heat (160° to 170°F) until melting, about 2 hours. Cool and reserve.

BABY TURNIPS

10 Japanese/Hakurei/baby turnips, scrubbed, stems removed
Kosher salt
125 grams turnipseed oil

Shave the turnips paper-thin on a mandoline or deli slicer. Season them with salt. Vacuum-seal the turnips and oil in a cryovac bag. Refrigerate until ready to use.

MORCILLA SAUCE

250 grams chopped morcilla
500 grams Dashi (recipe follows)
1.5 grams xanthan gum

1. In a blender, blend the morcilla and dashi on high speed for 1 minute.
2. Measure the morcilla-dashi mixture, then add 0.2% of that weight in xanthan gum (about 1.5 grams). Return the mixture to the blender and blend for 1 minute.
3. Using a ladle, pass the mixture through a chinois. Refrigerate until ready to use.

DASHI

55 grams dashi kombu
2.75 kilograms water
85 grams bonito flakes

1. Wipe the kombu with a damp cloth, then add it to the water in a medium pot and slowly bring to 146°F. Hold at this temperature for 1 hour.
2. Remove the kombu from the broth and bring the broth to 180°F.
3. Remove the pot from the heat. Add the bonito flakes and let them sink to the bottom of the pot (this will take several minutes). Let the broth sit for 10 more minutes, then strain through a chinois.
4. Cool and refrigerate until ready to use.

BONITA, SALSIFY, SEAWEED, PONZU, SESAME SEEDS

This dish is similar to the hamachi (page 47) in that it appears to be a piece of sushi nigiri. But here, salsify stands in for the rice.

At the time we created this, Ferran Adrià had already popularized spherification, the technique of trapping a liquid inside of a membrane. We never used alginate spheres, which were truly Ferran's territory; instead we used agar (a seaweed-based hydrocolloid) and locust bean gum (a common thickener found in cream cheese) to make beads of seaweed.

SERVES 8

8 quenelles Salsify "Rice" (page 54)

8 slices Bonita (page 54)

Ponzu Sauce (page 55)

"Caviar" Mix (page 55)

Grated lime zest

1. Warm the quenelles of salsify "rice" gently and quickly under a salamander.

2. On each plate, place a warmed quenelle. Place 1 slice of fish on top of the quenelle. Brush with ponzu. Top with a spoonful of "caviar" mix and garnish with lime zest.

SALSIFY "RICE"

Lemon juice or distilled white vinegar

10 salsify roots

2 grams kosher salt

5 grams hazelnut oil

Ultra-Sperse 3

1. Fill a bowl with cold water and add a squeeze of lemon or a dash of vinegar. Peel the salsify and cut into 2-inch plugs, dropping them immediately into the acidulated water to keep them from oxidizing. (This isn't supposed to be a piece of brown rice sushi.)
2. Drain the salsify, then vacuum-seal with the salt and hazelnut oil in a cryovac bag. Cook sous vide in a 158°F water bath for 25 minutes. Shock immediately in an ice bath.
3. In a food processor, pulse the salsify until it resembles grains of sushi rice.
4. Weigh the salsify and measure 5% of the total weight in Ultra-Sperse 3. Combine the two in a bowl and mix thoroughly with a spatula. Mold the mixture into sushi-rice quenelles.

BONITA

75 grams kosher salt

75 grams sugar

1 side bonita or mackerel (about 225 grams)

1. Combine the salt and sugar in a small bowl. Coat the fish liberally on both sides and let sit for 50 minutes. Rinse and pat dry.
2. Heat a plancha or cast-iron skillet over high heat; let it get very hot. Place the fish in the pan skin side down and cook, without touching, until the skin is charred, 30 seconds or less. Remove to a tray and chill in the refrigerator for at least 15 minutes, then slice thinly to order.

PONZU AND PONZU SAUCE

200 grams soy sauce

200 grams rice vinegar

150 grams mirin

35 grams lemon juice

35 grams lime juice

25 grams Dashi (page 51)

25 grams bonito flakes

Ultra-Sperse 3

1. Combine all of the ingredients in a large container and let stand for 24 hours. Strain out the bonito flakes.
2. Set aside 200 grams of the ponzu for marinating the trout roe (below right).
3. Weigh the remaining ponzu and measure 3% of that weight in Ultra-Sperse 3. Whisk the two together. This thickened ponzu sauce is used for dressing both the bonita and the "caviar" mix.

"CAVIAR" MIX

White Sesame Seed Caviar (recipe follows)

Seaweed Pearls (recipe follows)

Trout Roe (recipe follows)

2 to 3 tablespoons Ponzu Sauce (above)

Combine the sesame seed caviar, seaweed pearls, and marinated trout roe. Add just enough ponzu sauce to bring all of the beads together.

WHITE SESAME SEED CAVIAR

100 grams white sesame seeds

Water

Combine the sesame seeds and water to cover in a pressure cooker. Cook for 1 hour. Drain and cool.

SEAWEED PEARLS

150 grams rehydrated bright green wakame

100 grams cream cheese

600 grams water

4.5 grams kosher salt

No-boil agar

3 kilograms grapeseed oil

1. In a blender, process the rehydrated wakame with the cream cheese, water, and salt until smooth. Weigh the mixture, then mix in 0.9% of that weight in agar.
2. Pour the mixture into a saucepan and bring to 200°F, just below the boiling point, over high heat. Remove from the heat. Cool the mixture to 115°F and transfer to a squeeze bottle.
3. Place two one-third hotel pans over ice. In a stockpot, bring the grapeseed oil to 194°F, then pour into the hotel pans. The oil should be warm to the touch. Begin squeezing the seaweed mixture into the oil; the pearls will form as the mixture sinks to the bottom.
4. Let sit for 30 minutes. Strain the pearls and rinse under running water. Reserve the oil for another use.

TROUT ROE

200 grams trout roe

200 grams Ponzu (above left)

Marinate the trout roe in the ponzu for 12 hours.

CHICKEN LIVER, SICHUAN, INJERA, MELON

This started out as a foie gras dish when one of our cooks, Yoshi (David Yoshimura), wanted to create a heat-stable foie that he could char and serve with Sichuan peppercorn. At the time, we knew enough about gums and manipulating liver to execute the idea, but the end result was less than spectacular.

I helped Yoshi rethink the dish with chicken liver, which has more flavor than foie gras and plays well with other assertive flavors. We built the dish from there. I picked injera (Ethiopian bread) because I love the sourness of it, and I thought it would be fun to play with the texture. Melon brightened up the dish and gave it a friendly and approachable element.

When we plated it the first time we tried a schmear of the chicken liver, but we'd tried that look too many times. The chicken liver wasn't stable enough to cut into pieces, so I put it in a squeeze bottle one day, and out came the squiggles. Wylie particularly enjoyed this dish because he could write messages to familiar patrons in chicken liver. The notes were all somewhat obscene but always endearing, which is kind of how I feel about this dish.

—Sam Henderson, chef de cuisine

SERVES 8

Chicken Liver Mousse (page 58)
Melon Pickle (page 58)
Pickled Pearl Onions (page 58)
Toasted Injera (page 59)

Bitter greens, such as mustard greens or watercress
Melon Sauce (page 59)
Ground Sichuan peppercorns

1. Pipe some liver craziness onto each plate. Brûlé with a blowtorch.

2. Arrange 3 pieces of melon pickle, 3 pieces of pickled onions, 3 pieces of injera, and 3 leaves of the greens around the liver. Pool a few spoonfuls of the melon sauce within the folds of the liver squiggles. Dust with ground Sichuan pepper.

CHICKEN LIVER MOUSSE

500 grams chicken liver

Whole milk

2.5 grams Instacure #1

15 grams bourbon

2 grams Sichuan peppercorns

2 grams kosher salt, plus more to taste

Olive oil

1 small shallot, thinly sliced

1 clove garlic, thinly sliced

200 grams water

0.25 gram sodium hexametaphosphate

1.6 grams iota carrageenan

1.6 grams low-acyl gellan gum

1 gram calcium gluconate

1 gram sugar

125 grams melted butter, warm but not hot

1. Clean the liver—pick out any veins, pluck off any green bits of bile—and place in a clean container. Cover with milk and soak overnight.
2. In a small bowl, mix together the Instacure #1, bourbon, Sichuan peppercorns, and salt. Coat the liver on both sides with this mixture and let sit for 1 hour. Rinse and pat dry.
3. In a rondeau, heat a slick of olive oil over medium heat. Sweat the shallot and garlic until soft, about 10 minutes. Add the liver and sauté until cooked through, about 5 minutes. Set aside.
4. In a small saucepan, bring 100 grams of the water to a boil. Transfer to a blender quickly and shear in the gums in this order: sodium hexametaphosphate, carrageenan, and gellan. Let run for 10 seconds, then shear in the calcium and sugar. Set aside to cool.
5. In a blender, combine the cooked liver mixture and the remaining 100 grams water and purée until smooth. Add the hydrocolloid mixture to the blender and purée until smooth, then add the warm melted butter in a steady, slow stream. It may help to stop occasionally to scrape down the sides with a rubber spatula.
6. When finished, pass the liver mixture through a tamis and adjust the seasoning with a touch of additional salt if needed. Cool briefly, then transfer to a squeeze bottle.

MELON PICKLE

1 small honeydew melon

50 grams bottled yuzu juice

1 gram kosher salt

Cut one-half of the melon into ½-inch cubes. Juice the other half. Measure out 125 grams of juice and reserve for the Melon Sauce (page 59). Combine the melon cubes, 150 grams of melon juice, the yuzu juice, and salt in a cryovac bag and vacuum-seal. Refrigerate until ready to use.

PICKLED PEARL ONIONS

10 pearl onions, peeled and split into petals

75 grams distilled white vinegar

75 grams Champagne vinegar

2 grams kosher salt

38 grams sugar

1 bay leaf

1 sprig oregano

Place the onions in a heatproof nonreactive bowl or storage container. In a medium saucepan, combine the vinegars, salt, sugar, bay leaf, and oregano and bring to a boil. Pour the brine over the onions and cool. Refrigerate until ready to use.

TOASTED INJERA

1 injera pancake (we got ours from a local Ethiopian
   restaurant; you can also find them at some
   specialty stores)
Softened butter
Kosher salt
Ground Sichuan peppercorns

1. Cut the injera into small pennant-shaped triangles.
2. Before plating, place the triangles on a sizzle platter with a reasonable amount of tempered butter
   underneath. Dust the little flags lightly with salt
   and Sichuan peppercorns.
3. Toast under a salamander until they are crunchy-
   chewy, 2 to 3 minutes.

MELON SAUCE

125 grams honeydew melon juice (from Melon Pickle,
   page 58)
6 grams bottled yuzu juice
5 grams honey
1.25 grams kosher salt
1.1 grams xanthan gum

In a blender, process all of the ingredients on high
speed until smooth. Place the sauce in a 1-liter soda
bottle and connect to a CO_2 tank fitted with a gas
hose and soda bottle adapter. Carbonate according to
the tank's instructions. Once carbonated, decant the
melon sauce into a pint container and refrigerate until
ready to use.

COCONUT-SAFFRON ICE CREAM, CAVIAR, POPPY SEED

I love ice cream sandwiches, particularly the classic version with that amazing soft cookie and foamy vanilla ice cream. This caviar ice cream sandwich was an amuse-bouche from our later tasting-menu-only era. It was one of my all-time favorite amuses because ice cream and caviar are surprisingly delicious together. They seem like odd bedfellows, but to me, they're a logical pair: creamy and rich meets salty and briny.

SERVES 8

Coconut-Saffron Ice Cream (page 64)
8 Poppy Sables (page 64)
8 demitasse spoonfuls hackleback caviar

Epazote (shiso works well, too!)
Dried Lime (page 64)

1. Using a rolling pin, mold the ice cream between two silicone baking mats to about ½ inch in height. With a ring cutter, punch out 10 rounds of ice cream the same size as the poppy sable, and place each between 2 sables. Freeze quickly. Share the remaining ice cream with a friend.

2. In each bowl, place 1 spoonful of caviar. Set an ice cream sandwich on top. Then place a demitasse-size quenelle of caviar on top of the ice cream sandwich. Garnish with the epazote and dried lime.

COCONUT-SAFFRON ICE CREAM

5 egg yolks

8 grams sugar

25 grams powdered dextrose

400 grams coconut milk

0.75 gram saffron

0.8 gram xanthan gum

1.5 grams kosher salt

1. In a stand mixer fitted with the whisk attachment, whisk the yolks, sugar, and dextrose on high until creamy, 2 to 3 minutes.
2. Meanwhile, in a blender, combine the coconut milk and saffron. Shear in the xanthan gum and pass the mixture through a chinois into a saucepan.
3. Bring the coconut milk mixture to a boil and season it with the salt. With the mixer running, slowly temper the yolk mixture with the warm coconut milk.
4. Transfer the mixture to a double boiler and bring up to 160°F, whisking vigorously. Pass through a chinois and let cool.
5. Churn the mixture in an ice cream maker according to the manufacturer's instructions for a soft-serve consistency, usually about 5 minutes.

POPPY SABLE

80 grams poppy seeds

5 grams kosher salt

200 grams all-purpose flour

1.2 grams baking soda

170 grams butter

80 grams sugar

1. Heat the oven to 350°F.
2. In a blender, grind the poppy seeds, salt, flour, and baking soda to a fine powder. Set aside.
3. In a stand mixer fitted with the paddle attachment, cream the butter and sugar until pale, about 5 minutes. Beat the dry ingredients into the butter and sugar until combined.
4. Place a sheet of parchment paper on your counter and turn the dough out onto it. Place another sheet of parchment on top. Using a rolling pin, roll out the dough to ⅒ inch thick. Transfer to a sheet pan and bake for 7 minutes.
5. Punch out ¾-inch rounds while still warm (you'll get about 20). Let cool.

DRIED LIME

1 lime, thinly sliced

Dry the lime segments for 24 hours on an oiled dehydrator tray at 165°F. You'll know they're ready when they're black. Store in an airtight container until ready to use.

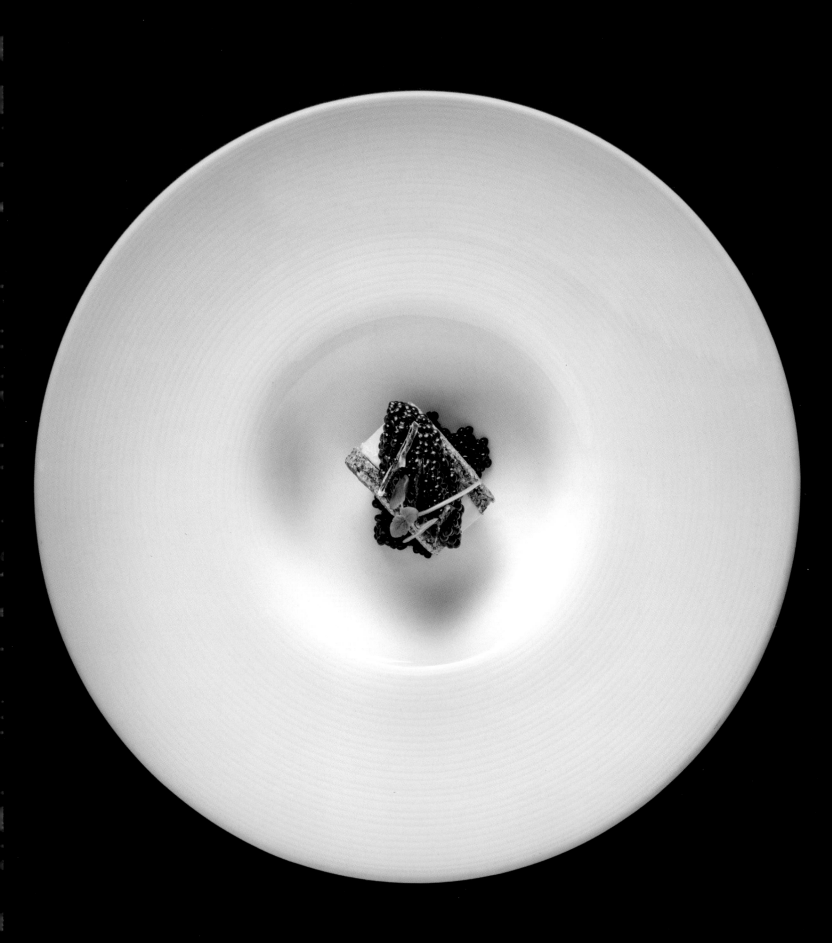

OYSTER IN ITS "SHELL," PRESERVED LEMON, HAZELNUT, SNOW PEAS

Watching people eat this dish was always fun. They had to get over a psychological hurdle before they dug in, because they knew they weren't supposed to eat an oyster shell. Our goal wasn't to stump people, although we did enjoy stumping other chefs. Even the smart ones, the ones who know the tricks, would come in and say, "Huh?"

To create the shell, we built on the technique we used for the Poached Egg, Edible Shell (page 83), but the original inspiration came from Andoni Aduriz's potato stones at Spain's renowned Mugartiz. He dips cooked stone-size potatoes in a batter made from edible clay, and when the potatoes dry, they look exactly like little stones. It's magically disorienting to eat them.

The first time I tried that dish, I wondered what I could do with edible clay that wouldn't be a direct copy of Andoni's stones. Finally it dawned on me: Rather than dip something in the clay, I could use the shell to make an empty casing. Andoni was kind enough to share the recipe, and we modified it a bit for the original egg dish and for this hazelnut-flavored variation.

SERVES 8

Preserved Lemon Gel (page 68)

8 Oyster "Shells" (page 68)

1 dozen Shigoku oysters, shucked and stored in their liquor

Pickled Shallots (page 69)

Snow Peas (page 69)

Hazelnut–Toasted Milk Solids (page 69)

Into each bowl, pipe or spoon a small amount (roughly 2 grams) of lemon gel. Place a "shell" on top of the gel and cradle an oyster in its lap as though it were being served in the half-shell. Lay a few pieces of pickled shallot and snow pea on top, then scatter a demitasse spoonful of milk solids to the side to finish.

PRESERVED LEMON GEL

30 grams Preserved Lemon (page 50)

50 grams sugar

100 grams lemon juice

5.8 grams (1%) agar

400 grams water

1. In a blender, process the preserved lemon, sugar, and lemon juice for 1 minute, or until the mixture comes together. (If it does not totally homogenize, don't worry: You are reblending and passing the gel in step 4.)
2. Separately, in a blender, shear the agar into the water. Transfer to a small pot, bring to a boil, and simmer for 5 minutes.
3. In a separate pot, bring the lemon mixture to a boil. Whisk in the boiling water mixture, then pour the gel into a metal pan set over an ice bath. Let cool until firm.
4. In a small blender, blend the gel, then pass through a chinois. Refrigerate until ready to use. This will produce more than you need, but you have to make at least this amount so the mixture will blend properly.

OYSTER "SHELLS"

The magic of this dish is made possible by American-made edible clay. If you are familiar with Kaopectate, the K-A-O is for kaolin, the name of the clay; it helps calm your stomach. Some people get concerned when they hear you're serving them clay, but it's incredibly safe, and humans have been consuming clay for millennia.

150 grams Kaolin Base (recipe follows)

50 grams hazelnut oil

15 grams butter, melted

0.45 gram (0.3%) xanthan gum

25 grams unseasoned squid ink

Cooking spray

1. Preheat a convection oven to 200°F.
2. Place the kaolin base in a blender and, with the machine running, stream in the oil and melted butter at low speed. Shear in the xanthan gum. Transfer the mixture to a small bowl and gently and irregularly fold in the squid ink—the colors should not homogenize.
3. Coat 12 small madeleine molds with cooking spray and cut out twelve ½-inch squares of parchment.
4. Spoon one demitasse of the clay-ink mixture into each mold. Coat one side of the parchment squares with cooking spray and place on top of the mixture. Press to distribute over the mold and place a few dried beans on top for weight. Bake until crunchy, 30 to 40 minutes.

KAOLIN BASE

70 grams kaolin (edible clay)

25 grams maltodextrin

5.25 grams egg white powder

25 grams Hazelnut–Toasted Milk Solids (below)

105 grams water

In a blender, process the kaolin, maltodextrin, egg white powder, and toasted milk solids. Pass through a tamis into a bowl. Whisk in the water and cover with plastic wrap for 20 minutes to hydrate. The kaolin base can be held for up to 1 week in the refrigerator.

PICKLED SHALLOTS

1 large shallot, thinly shaved

100 grams Champagne vinegar

50 grams water

50 grams sugar

5 grams kosher salt

5 grams tarragon leaves

1 clove garlic

Place the shaved shallot in a heatproof plastic container. In a small pot, combine the remaining ingredients and bring to a boil. Pour the brine over the shallot. Refrigerate at least overnight or until ready to use. Discard the tarragon and garlic before serving.

SNOW PEAS

Kosher salt

1 liter water

10 snow peas, stemmed and strings removed

Bring a small pot of salted water to a boil. Blanch the peas until tender but still crunchy, about 3 minutes. Shock in ice water and pat dry. Chiffonade. Refrigerate until ready to use.

HAZELNUT-TOASTED MILK SOLIDS

225 grams hazelnut oil

60 grams nonfat milk powder

Kosher salt

1. Put the oil in a small pot and bring it to 200°F over medium-low heat.
2. Whisk in the milk powder, slowly bringing up the temperature of the oil. It should not pass 300°F. Toast the milk solids to a light golden brown, 8 to 10 minutes, stirring constantly.
3. Strain the solids out of the oil and transfer them to paper towels. Change the paper towels several times to prevent the solids from reabsorbing the fat and becoming greasy. Season with salt.

(THE ONLY SALAD)

We never offered salad at wd~50. I've just never found joy in eating it. I like oil and vinegar as ingredients. I like the assorted things that you might find in a salad: herbs, radicchio, watercress, endive, romaine. I just don't like a bowl of them tossed with dressing. Customers, especially in the early years, often felt differently. The poor waitstaff. Every night they would come back and plead, "Table 10 wants to know if they can have a salad."

"I'm sorry, they can't," I would say. "They cannot have a salad."

"But we had salad for staff meal today, chef. Can't we do something for them?"

"We cannot."

My argument was: We have eighteen carefully thought-out items on the menu. If a customer doesn't want one of them, there are approximately 18,000 other restaurants in the city, many of which serve salad. And those restaurants don't have what we serve here. If you go to the salad restaurant and tell them *I'd like to have fried mayonnaise,* they will say I'm sorry, we don't offer that.

Tim Zagat, patriarch of the Zagat guides, came to wd~50 in the early days with a companion who wanted a salad. The Zagats weren't used to hearing the word "no," and when Tim left that night, he came to the kitchen, gave me a Zagat guide, and told me that within six months I would be serving salad. This just confirmed we would never do it.

Now, there's saying no to everyone, and then there's saying no to Lou Reed. He and I won "New Yorkers of the Year" awards from *New York* magazine when I was at 71 Clinton. After the event, he started coming to 71 and then to wd~50, and he always wanted things that we didn't serve, like cooked greens or salad. And we'd find some pea shoots to sauté. It was Lou effing Reed, the coolest person who was ever going to come for dinner, so I figured, let's meet him halfway.

One day, shortly before a visit from Lou, we were messing around with egg white powder. Normally we would reconstitute it by whisking it with water, but we were wondering what else would work. Beet juice did all kinds of cool things, and then I tried vinegar and it worked beautifully. I thought, *Okay, whipped vinegar? Why not add oil and make a whipped vinaigrette?* It was like a meringue, basically. When Lou Reed came in that night, asking as usual for a salad, I dunked an endive leaf into the whipped vinaigrette and blasted the meringue with a torch, which gave it a marshmallow-just-out-of-the-fire texture. I seasoned it with a touch of tomato powder and out it went: the only "salad" we ever served.

It embodied all the elements of a salad. It had a crispy water-y thing, it had a tomato product, it had oil and vinegar. I'm not sure why we didn't say, *Okay, everybody. We're doing a salad now.* I think I was just too stubborn. I did make it once for Sean Brock years later, and then I put it on the menu the last two weeks wd~50 was open. After a dozen years, I guess I was almost ready to serve something somewhat like a salad.

EGGS

EGGS BENEDICT

Eggs Benedict—the original, the one served at every brunch everywhere—is a stroke of genius. I mean, eggs covered by eggs! When I'm eating it, all is right with the world.

This dish goes back to one of the early hits at the restaurant: beef tongue with deep-fried mayonnaise. It was on our menu in 2004 and people came back asking for it until we closed. But the secret of our fried mayonnaise (as explained on page 32) is that there are no eggs in it.

By 2007, we'd learned a lot about egg sauces, emulsions, and gum technology, and we thought, *We've got to be able to fry a sauce with eggs in it.* So we set out to fry hollandaise, one of the first sauces I learned to make. There are many days when I forget where I parked my car, but I will always remember that nine yolks and a pound of butter equals a good hollandaise.

We often look backward to go forward, so before we started experimenting, we thought about traditional egg-based sauces in which the yolk gets really hot. Pastry cream is an obvious one. Why does pastry cream work? Why can you boil it without scrambling the eggs? The key ingredient is cornstarch—there's a ton of starch in pastry cream, and that insulates the emulsion. So we added a modified cornstarch to our hollandaise, along with gellan gum, to help the sauce withstand high temperatures. We also added a little gelatin, so we could cut the chilled sauce into cubes before we fried it. I liked that it looked like a fried crouton but would ooze hollandaise when you cut into it.

Once we had fryable hollandaise, the dish came together pretty easily. We already had the perfect egg yolk to serve with it: About a year before, we had created a dish for a European book series by Patrick Mikanowski that included an egg yolk cooked slowly in a plastic sleeve. The result was a tube of egg yolk with a texture somewhere between cheese and fudge. To incorporate the requisite English muffins and ham, we dried and ground English muffins into breading for the hollandaise cubes, and we cut paper-thin slices of ham and dried them in the oven. With a sprinkle of chive and black salt (which looks like pepper), it was ready to go.

SERVES 8

Neutral oil, for deep-frying

16 cubes frozen Hollandaise Cubes
    (page 79)

24 Egg Yolks (page 80), warmed

24 pieces Canadian Bacon (page 80)

24 chive points

Black sea salt (from Cyprus)

1. Heat the oven to 200°F. Heat a large pot of oil to 375°F.

2. Fry the frozen hollandaise cubes to a golden brown, a minute or two. Place on a sheet pan and bake until a cake tester inserted into the center feels warm to the touch, about 2 minutes.

3. Build the dish: Arrange 3 plugs of egg yolk in a somewhat circular arrangement. One should be standing straight up, the other 2 should be laid on their sides, their tail ends smushed and dragged, to suggest a circle. Place a cube of hollandaise on the end of each schmear. Garnish with bacon crisps, chives, and black sea salt. Serve immediately.

HOLLANDAISE CUBES

GELLAN BASE
170 grams water

0.68 gram sodium hexametaphosphate

3.4 grams low-acyl gellan gum

1.7 grams calcium lactate

ULTRA-SPERSE MIXTURE
110 grams water

10 grams Ultra-Sperse M

GELATIN MIXTURE
60 grams silver sheet gelatin, soaked in ice water
for 5 to 10 minutes, taking care to separate the
sheets

640 grams butter, melted (at least 99°F)

HOLLANDAISE CUBES
100 grams egg yolks

Kosher salt

Lemon juice

75 grams all-purpose flour

1 egg, beaten

75 grams panko breadcrumbs or toasted English
muffin crumbs, ground to a powder

1. Make the gellan base: In a blender, blend the water and sodium hexametaphosphate until smooth, then blend in the gellan. Pour the mixture into a saucepan and bring to a boil. Add the calcium lactate and bring back to a boil. Pour into a container and cool until set. It should be the texture of firm Jell-O.

2. Make the Ultra-Sperse mixture: In a large bowl, whisk together the water and Ultra-Sperse. Set aside.

3. Make the gelatin mixture: Whisk together the gelatin and melted butter until the gelatin dissolves.

4. In a medium bowl, whisk together the Ultra-Sperse mixture and half of the gelatin mixture. Set the

Ultra-Sperse/gelatin and the remaining plain gelatin aside.

5. Make the hollandaise cubes: Blend the gellan base and the egg yolks until smooth. With the motor running, slowly pour in the reserved plain gelatin mixture in a steady, continuous stream, then pour in the Ultra-Sperse/gelatin mixture. At this point, you should have a thick, creamy sauce. Adjust the seasoning with salt and lemon juice.

6. Line a 4-inch-deep one-sixth sheet pan (6 x 7 x 4 inches) with plastic. Pour the hollandaise mixture into the pan and refrigerate overnight.

7. Place the flour, beaten egg, and breadcrumbs in separate bowls.

8. Cut the hollandaise into 1-centimeter cubes. Coat each cube with the flour, then the egg wash, then the breadcrumbs. Place in a single layer on a sheet pan and cover with plastic wrap. Freeze until ready to use.

EGG YOLKS

10 egg yolks
1 pinch kosher salt
1 pinch cayenne pepper
Cooking spray

1. In a large bowl, combine the egg yolks, salt, and cayenne and mix with an immersion blender until evenly seasoned.
2. Using a soup funnel, fill two ⅓ x 12-inch plastic sleeves with the yolk mixture and tie the tops with string to secure. Prop them upright in the refrigerator for 2 hours to allow any air to rise to the top. Pull from the fridge and let sit at room temperature for 30 minutes.
3. Set up a 165°F water bath in a tall bain-marie or other container that will keep the yolk sleeves standing upright. Add the sleeves, turn the temperature down to 158°F, and cook for 17 minutes. Place the sleeves in an ice water bath. Chill for at least 30 minutes. Refrigerate overnight.
4. Line a half-sheet pan with parchment and coat the parchment with cooking spray. Slice open the sleeves, remove the yolks, and cut into 1-inch-long plugs. Arrange them on the prepared sheet pan, wrap in plastic, and refrigerate.
5. When ready to serve, gently warm in a low oven for 6 to 8 minutes. (We used a CVap set to 125°F.) Set aside.

CANADIAN BACON

100 grams Canadian bacon, frozen

Thinly shave the bacon on a deli slicer. Lay on dehydrator mats and dry at 160°F until red and crispy, about 30 minutes. Hold at room temperature until ready to use.

HOW THE SLOW-POACHED EGG CAME TO CLINTON STREET

During one of my trips to the Lo Mejor de la Gastronomía conference in the Basque part of Spain, I stopped to eat at Josean Alija's restaurant at the Guggenheim Bilbao and he served us a slow-poached egg in red pepper water. Later that week, chef Andoni Aduriz at Mugaritz served us a slow-poached egg with truffled breadcrumbs in a hen consommé. I was blown away. I had never seen eggs cooked like this. Slow-poached eggs—cooked in their shells, so they still have that iconic egg shape, but with the texture of the runniest poached eggs imaginable—are everywhere these days, but at the time they seemed very new.

When I got home and researched the method, I learned that the technique comes from the famous *onsen* egg of Japan. Onsens are hot springs, and for centuries, the Japanese have been sliding baskets full of eggs onto the ends of bamboo sticks, lowering them into the water, and letting the slow, steady, not-quite-boiling heat of the spring cook the eggs. In Spain, chefs were using a water bath, kept warm by an immersion circulator, to create that environment. In the end, we cooked ours the same way but a little hotter than what was in vogue in Europe, because I like the white of the egg a little firmer.

POACHED EGG, EDIBLE SHELL, CAESAR, PUMPERNICKEL

This was the first dish we served in which we used kaolin clay to make an edible shell. The edible oyster shell (page 68) was the second iteration of the technique.

We added a Caesar dressing, because I think it makes just about anything irresistible—even something seemingly inedible.

SERVES 6

6 Six-Minute Eggs (page 84)

Caesar Dressing (page 84)

3-2-1 Pickled Lily Bulbs (page 84)

12 Pumpernickel Toasts (page 84)

12 Edible Eggshells (page 85)

Olive oil

Maldon salt

6 sprigs chervil

1. Fill a large saucepan with water and place over medium heat. Gently warm the eggs in the water.

2. For each plate, use a small offset spatula to drag about 1 tablespoon of dressing across the plate in a rectangular shape. Scatter a few lily bulb petals on top. Place an egg in the center of the Caesar dressing, then arrange 2 pieces of pumpernickel toast and 2 eggshells around the egg. Season the egg with olive oil and Maldon salt and garnish with a sprig of chervil.

SIX-MINUTE EGGS

2 kilograms water
15 grams distilled white vinegar
15 grams kosher salt
6 eggs

1. In a large saucepan, bring the water to a boil over high heat and add the vinegar and salt. Carefully drop in the eggs and cook for 6 minutes. Shock immediately in an ice bath. Let cool.
2. Peel and store on paper towels until ready to use.

CAESAR DRESSING

50 grams lemon juice
2 anchovy fillets, rinsed well
½ clove garlic, slivered
1 egg yolk
0.5 gram freshly ground black pepper
50 grams Parmesan cheese, grated
50 grams water
22.5 grams Worcestershire sauce
1.5 grams PGA
125 grams olive oil
125 grams grapeseed oil
Kosher salt

1. In a blender, process the lemon juice, anchovies, garlic, egg yolk, black pepper, Parmesan, water, and Worcestershire sauce until smooth. Add the PGA and blend again for 10 seconds.
2. With the motor running, stream in the olive oil and grapeseed oil. Blend until emulsified. Season with salt. Refrigerate until ready to use.

3-2-1 PICKLED LILY BULBS

2 lily bulbs, broken into petals and rinsed
350 grams rice vinegar
240 grams water
100 grams sugar
6 grams kosher salt

Place the lily bulb petals in a heatproof bowl or container. In a saucepan, bring the vinegar, water, sugar, and salt to a boil and pour over the petals. Refrigerate overnight and until ready to use.

PUMPERNICKEL TOAST

Super–thinly sliced and toasted bread can be a great textural addition to a dish, but the bread needs to be flavorful. Frozen, shaved, baked, and dried brioche always has a great texture, but when it's paper-thin, you can't taste that great yeasty flavor. Pumpernickel has a complex, molasses, rye-rich flavor that shows up to the party, any way you slice it.

½ loaf pumpernickel bread
115 grams butter, melted
Kosher salt

1. Remove the crust from the pumpernickel and freeze the loaf.
2. Heat the oven to 200°F.
3. Shave the frozen loaf on a deli slicer on setting #1 through the width of the bread. Cut the slices into 3 x 2-inch rectangles. Brush the rectangles with butter and sprinkle with salt.
4. Crumple foil into uneven shapes, enough to cover a half-sheet pan. (A tuile mold may also be used.) Lay the bread over the top of the foil and bake until crispy, about 15 minutes. Hold at room temperature until ready to use.

EDIBLE EGGSHELLS

This recipe makes enough clay mixture for a couple dozen shells. The shell-making process can be somewhat frustrating until you get the hang of it—the shells can break and stick—so these amounts allow for a bit of practice.

140 grams kaolin (edible clay)

50 grams Maltrin 500 (maltodextrin)

10.5 grams egg white powder

50 grams Brown Butter Solids (below right)

210 grams water

12 to 15 small water balloons

12 to 15 skewers

Styrofoam brick

1. In a blender, process the kaolin, maltodextrin, egg white powder, and brown butter solids, then pass through a tamis into a large bowl. Whisk in the water, cover, and set aside for 20 minutes to hydrate.
2. Blow up the water balloons until they are slightly larger than an egg. Dip the balloons halfway into the clay mixture, shaking a few times to remove any excess. You're looking for a thin layer. Pierce each balloon through its knot with a skewer, then stand the skewers in a Styrofoam base. Store in a dry area overnight.
3. The next day, deflate the balloons: Pinch the balloon just above the knot, then use a cake tester to poke between the knot and where you are pinching the balloon. Control the air coming out to deflate the balloon slowly; if you deflate it too quickly or pop it, the shells will crack. Store the shells in cardboard egg cartons until ready to use.

BROWN BUTTER SOLIDS

450 grams butter, melted

125 grams nonfat milk powder

1. Place the melted butter in a medium saucepan and place over medium heat. Whisk in the milk powder, continuing to whisk as the butter comes to between 250° and 300°F. Once all of the water has evaporated, the milk solids will begin browning.
2. Once the solids are golden brown, strain the mixture through a chinois and pat the solids down on paper towels. Let cool, changing the paper towels several times so the solids don't reabsorb the fat. Store in a plastic container at room temperature until ready to use.

SCRAMBLED EGG RAVIOLI, CHARRED AVOCADO, KINDAI KAMPACHI

I don't know exactly why I set out to make scrambled eggs in the shape of a cube. I'm drawn to bold, graphic shapes, and I just thought square food would be fun for a change. Also, I can't imagine anything better than egg wrapped in egg. The idea came from a dish I tried at Falai (one of our neighboring Clinton Street restaurants): agnolotti with scrambled eggs inside.

The scrambled egg filling was fairly simple: 4 parts egg, 1 part cream cheese (I always make my scrambled eggs with cream cheese, so this wasn't any great leap of faith), and a little gelatin, so we could set the filling in molds and cut them into big blocky cubes. The tricky part was figuring out how to make a wrapper out of eggs.

We tried almost every gum and technique in our modern-cooking arsenal, and then a funny thing happened: One of the leaders of modernist cooking showed up and said, "Why don't you just dip the cubes in egg yolks?" He was Oriol Castro, the brains behind a lot of the savory food at el Bulli during its last fifteen years. He came to work with us for a week as part of an exchange I'd arranged with Ferran Adrià, and the timing was perfect. We did what Oriol suggested and started dipping the scrambled egg center in egg yolk and then slipping it into hot water. It almost worked, but the yolk wrapper kept sliding off.

Why wouldn't the wrapper stay put? We noticed that in the time between when we popped the frozen egg cube out of the mold and when we slipped it into the water, the change in temperature caused it to frost—much like when you pull a glass out of the freezer and it instantly turns frosty. The solution: We started dipping the cubes in hot water for a split second, just to remove that frost layer, then we patted them dry, which made them almost tacky. We added a little xanthan gum to the yolks, which gave them enough viscosity to cling right to the scrambled eggs.

There was an art to dunking the cubes in the yolk—they were each on a skewer, and coating them was almost like chocolate-making. The process was temperamental: The water had to be just below a boil so the coating wouldn't blow off. We needed the cubes to bob like buoys out at sea. And we needed them to do this for exactly long enough to cook the wrapper without further cooking the eggs inside. Oddly enough, for all the science that went into this dish, we knew they were done in the water when the skewer came out easily. It was a little funny to give the cooks in the kitchen all these technical instructions and then, when they asked how they'd know the eggs were done, we'd say, "Oh, when the stick comes out!"

When we served the dish it was a beautiful, perfectly square omelet, filled with soft-curd scrambled eggs. We served it with a brunoise of potatoes, brûléed avocado, and kampachi.

SERVES 4

4 Scrambled Egg Ravioli (page 89)

Avocado Purée (page 90)

Fried Potato Dice (page 90)

8 slices Kindai Kampachi (page 90)

Sea salt

Olive oil

1. Heat a saucepan of water to 170°F. Warm the ravioli in the water until a cake tester inserted into the center is warm to the touch, about 5 minutes.

2. On each plate, pipe a 2-inch-long cylinder of avocado purée and brûlée with a blowtorch. Place a warmed ravioli on one side of the purée and pile a teaspoon of the diced potato on the other.

3. Top the ravioli with 2 slices of the fish. Finish with sea salt and olive oil.

SCRAMBLED EGG RAVIOLI

About 4 liters water, for cooking

385 grams egg yolks

15 grams water

0.3 gram xanthan gum

Kosher salt

Cayenne pepper

Scrambled Egg Cubes (recipe follows)

1. In a stockpot, bring the 4 liters of water to a simmer and hold at around 175°F.
2. In a blender on very low speed (no higher than setting #2 on a Vitamix), blend the egg yolks, 15 grams of water, xanthan gum, and salt and cayenne to taste. You will see a vortex appear. When the vortex pops, or inverts, stop blending. This is the "egg dip." Refrigerate overnight to allow air to rise to the top. Bring to room temperature for 30 minutes before using.
3. Individually impale each egg cube with a skewer. Submerge in the simmering water very briefly, then pat down with a paper towel. This ensures the egg dip will adhere.
4. Carefully drag a cube through the dip, then tap off the excess yolk. Gently place the cube into simmering water. After about 1 minute, the cube will fall from the skewer. Cook for another 90 seconds after this happens to ensure that the yolk coating is completely cooked. Place in an ice bath if serving later, or reserve in warm water if serving right away. Repeat for the remaining cubes.

SCRAMBLED EGG CUBES

100 grams eggs

Kosher salt

Cayenne pepper

5 grams butter

25 grams cream cheese, at room temperature

2 grams silver sheet gelatin, bloomed in ice water

1. In a small bowl, whisk the eggs with a pinch each of salt and cayenne.
2. In a small saucepan, melt the butter over low heat. Pour in the eggs and stir constantly (we used a heart-shaped whisk) for 10 minutes to create very fine curds. When the eggs are finished, the consistency should resemble cooked oatmeal.
3. Take the eggs off the heat and whisk in the cream cheese and gelatin. Place the mixture in a pastry bag and pipe into 4 cubes in a 1¼-inch silicone ice cube mold. Take care to pipe into the corners of the mold, pressing the mixture with a small offset spatula so the cubes are nice and sharp. Cover with plastic wrap and freeze.
4. Once frozen, pop the cubes out of the mold and store in a plastic container in the freezer.

AVOCADO PURÉE

250 grams avocados (about 2)

25 grams plain Greek yogurt

25 grams Dijon mustard

0.5 gram sodium bisulfite

Lemon juice

Kosher salt

6 grams (2%) Ultra-Sperse 3

1. Scoop the avocados into a blender and purée until smooth. Pass through a tamis into a large bowl.
2. Mix in the yogurt, mustard, sodium bisulfite, and lemon juice and salt to taste. Whisk in the Ultra-Sperse 3.
3. Transfer the mixture to a pastry bag fitted with a ¾-inch tip. Refrigerate until ready to serve.

FRIED POTATO DICE

Very tiny, very crisp potatoes were an important textural element in this dish. You need to soak them in water first to remove the starch, which will help them fry up crisp and not burn. (You might accidentally burn them anyway; they're so impossibly small that they'll be goners before you realize it.)

We used a deep fryer, but you could also shallow-fry them in a pan: Drop your potatoes in and have a sieve and a heatproof container nearby. Lift the pan off the heat before you think the potatoes are done—it won't even take 2 minutes—and pour the oil out into the container, catching your potatoes in the sieve. Then lay them out on paper towels to absorb the extra oil, and season them lightly.

1 russet potato, peeled, brunoised, and rinsed

Neutral oil, for deep-frying

Kosher salt

1. As you work, drop the potato dice into a large bowl of water. Let soak for 30 minutes to remove the starch. Drain well and pat very dry.
2. Heat a pot of oil to 300°F.
3. Place the potato dice in a chinois (to act as a frying basket), lower into the hot oil, and fry, stirring constantly, until crispy, 3 to 4 minutes. Dump out onto paper towels, spreading the potatoes out to keep them crisp. Season with salt.

KINDAI KAMPACHI

170 grams Kindai kampachi fillet

153 grams sugar

128 grams kosher salt

500 grams rice vinegar

25 grams soy sauce

1. Rub the fish with 128 grams of the sugar and place in a small baking dish. Refrigerate for 40 minutes.
2. Rinse the sugar off the fish and pat dry. Repeat the same process with the salt, refrigerating for 1 hour.
3. In a large bowl, whisk together the vinegar, soy sauce, and remaining 25 grams of sugar.
4. Rinse the salt off the fish and place the fish in the marinade. Refrigerate for 20 minutes, flipping the fish halfway through.
5. Rinse the marinade off the fish and slice into 8 thin slices. Refrigerate the slices until ready to use.

EGG YOLK–MASHED POTATO RAVIOLI, CAVIAR, CUCUMBER

This is like the black-tie version of Scrambled Egg Ravioli (page 89). The execution is different, but the conceit (eggs as wrapper) is the same.

SERVES 6 TO 8

12 to 16 Egg Yolk–Mashed Potato Ravioli (page 94)

Egg Sauce (see page 94, step 1)

60 to 80 grams grinnell caviar (or tonburi, for vegetarians)

Cucumber Sauce (page 95)

Sea salt

Cucumber Brunoise (page 95)

Fried Potato Dice (page 90)

Micro arugula

1. Reheat the ravioli in a CVap oven at 125°F for at least 6 minutes. When the ravioli are ready, they will take on the shape of small pillows.

2. Place the bottle of egg sauce in a bain-marie to warm through.

3. In a small bowl, dress the caviar with cucumber sauce.

4. On each plate, place two very small piles of cucumber across the plate from each other, then place 1 ravioli on top of each cucumber pile. Dress each with some of the warm egg sauce and some sea salt. Spoon about 10 grams of the caviar in an arc around the ravioli. Garnish with fried potato dice and micro arugula.

EGG YOLK–MASHED POTATO RAVIOLI

EGG SAUCE AND WRAPPERS
Egg Base (recipe follows)

POTATO FILLING
1 large russet potato, scrubbed
2 sprigs thyme
1 bay leaf
1 clove garlic
10 grams kosher salt, plus more for seasoning
35 grams heavy cream
10 grams butter
10 grams (4%) silver sheet gelatin,
    bloomed in ice water
White pepper

1. Make the egg sauce: Measure out 2 tablespoons of the egg base and place in a very small squeeze bottle, putting plastic wrap underneath the top before you screw it on. Place the bottle in a cryovac bag, but do not seal it. Submerge the bag, with a small weight to keep it down, in a 147°F water bath and cook for 5 minutes. Cool in an ice bath.

2. Make the egg wrappers: Cut two sheets of acetate to the dimensions of a half-sheet pan and place one sheet in the pan. Spread the remainder of the egg base in a paper-thin layer on top of the first sheet of acetate, then place the second sheet on top. Cook in a CVap oven at 165°F for 17 minutes.

3. Place a layer of plastic wrap over the top sheet of acetate and pour ice on top of it. Let cool for at least 10 minutes.

4. Cut the cooked egg sheets into 8.5 x 6-centimeter rectangles.

5. Make the potato filling: In a small stockpot, combine the potato, thyme, bay leaf, garlic, water to cover, and salt and bring to a simmer. Cook until the potato is tender, 20 to 30 minutes. When cool enough to handle, peel the potato and run it through a ricer. Weigh out 200 grams of cooked potato and transfer to a bowl.

6. In a small saucepan, warm the cream and butter over medium heat. Whisk in the gelatin.

7. Fold the cream mixture into the potatoes. Pass through a tamis and season with salt and white pepper. Pour the mixture onto a one-sixth sheet pan lined with parchment paper. Cool over an ice bath until firm to the touch.

8. Cut into rectangular 1 x 2 x 2.5-centimeter planks.

9. Assemble the ravioli: Place a potato portion in the middle of each egg sheet and wrap tightly, like a gift. Pull the longer sides of the sheet over each other, and then do the same with the shorter sides, pressing against the potato as you go. (If the ravioli are not wrapped tightly, they will fall apart once warmed.) Refrigerate until ready to use.

EGG BASE

250 grams egg yolks
1 gram kosher salt
0.5 gram (0.2%) xanthan gum
1 pinch cayenne pepper

Blend all the ingredients together until smooth, then compress the mixture in a cryovac machine to remove any air. You can do this in any open container; we used a hotel pan. Repeat the process twice to ensure all the air is out of the emulsion.

CUCUMBER SAUCE

120 grams cucumber juice

20 grams diced cucumber, skin on

0.4 gram kosher salt

0.5 gram Honey Garlic (page 26)

1.5 grams honey

0.1 gram citric acid

0.56 gram xanthan gum

Blend all the ingredients together until smooth, then pass through a chinois. Place in an ice bath to cool.

CUCUMBER BRUNOISE

1 English hothouse cucumber, peeled, seeded, and brunoised

Olive oil

Kosher salt

Place the cucumber in a small bowl and dress with olive oil and salt.

CARROT-COCONUT "SUNNY-SIDE UP"

This dish is like a showcase for gums: locust bean gum, guar gum, and xanthan gum, plus carrageenan. The white of the egg is coconut milk infused with cardamom and seasoned with sugar, then passed and blended with the gums. Individually, locust bean, guar, and xanthan can only thicken a liquid, not make a gel. Together, though, they have great synergy: The combination ends up mimicking the texture of cooked egg white.

The yolk is carrot juice blended with smoked maple syrup, salt, a little glucose (to keep it from freezing solid in the molds), and some xanthan gum to give it the viscosity of a proper egg yolk. After it's frozen, it goes into a warm bath of kappa carrageenan and locust bean gum to make a gel membrane around it. Then as the iced carrot juice thaws, it's contained in the membrane and behaves like a yolk.

We finished it with salt, a crack of pepper, and a drizzle of olive oil: a carrot coconut sunny-side up.

SERVES 8

Coconut "Egg White" (page 98)   Olive oil
Carrot "Yolk" (page 98)
Kosher salt and freshly ground black
    pepper

1. On each plate, pour an "egg white" as directed (page 98).

2. Coat a "yolk" as directed (page 98) and place on top of the egg white. Set aside until the "yolk" thaws—it will take about 30 minutes. If the yolk weeps, blot with a paper towel.

3. Season with salt, pepper, and olive oil and serve.

COCONUT "EGG WHITE"

500 grams coconut milk

9 grams black cardamom pods, cracked

20 grams sugar

0.8 gram xanthan gum

0.8 gram locust bean gum

0.8 gram guar gum

1. In a bowl, combine the coconut milk, cardamom, and sugar. Steep for 20 minutes, then strain into a saucepan.
2. Heat the mixture to 180°F. Whisk in all the gums, blending thoroughly.
3. Ladle about 50 grams of milk onto each plate or sauté pan. Work fast, as the mixture will set quickly.

CARROT "YOLK"

250 grams carrot juice

25 grams glucose powder

Smoked Maple Syrup (page 313)

Kosher salt

1.5 grams xanthan gum

Egg Yolk Membrane (recipe follows), at 115°F

1. In a blender, process the carrot juice, glucose, maple syrup, and salt until smooth. Add the xanthan gum and blend again. Refrigerate the carrot mixture for at least 1 hour to settle; skim off any foam that has risen to the top. Pour the mixture into 1-inch-diameter demisphere molds and freeze.
2. When ready to plate, use a toothpick to lift a "yolk" from its mold and dip in the pan of warm egg membrane. Let sit for 2 to 3 minutes, until coated. Then plate immediately.

EGG YOLK MEMBRANE

250 grams water

1 gram locust bean gum

1 gram kappa carrageenan

0.12 gram potassium chloride

Blend all the ingredients together and pour into a saucepan. Heat to 180°F, then cool to 115°F.

SOUP

MUSSEL OLIVE OIL SOUP

Originally, we would steam the mussels for this soup the usual way, with shallots, white wine, thyme, garlic, and bay leaves. One of my all-time favorite cooks, Fran Derby, would put beautiful French Mauviel copper pots on the flattop, and then go on a walkabout until the pots were ripping hot. Then he'd throw the mussels and some white wine in them, slam the cover, and the mussels would steam open instantly. Over time, the pans all buckled from the repetitive thermal shock. Lucky for Fran, I didn't discover this until long after the dish was off the menu.

Once the mussels were steamed open, we'd purée them, along with aromatics and olive oil and end up with a decadent soup that was, unfortunately, army-green and not the best-looking thing on the menu. We needed to garnish it, but we never wanted to pour the soup tableside; that would have felt too formal. Instead we created a garnish that appeared to be floating on top of the soup.

We used squares of water chestnuts as pedestals for steamed mussels: We cryovaced them with Chinese black vinegar beforehand, because water chestnuts have almost no flavor on their own, and the soup needed some acid to cut through the richness of the mussels and olive oil.

SERVES 4

150 grams sake, plus more as needed

1 kilogram mussels, scrubbed

12 water chestnuts, cut into 1¼ x ½ x ¼-inch rectangles

Chinese black vinegar

425 grams Spanish olive oil (or another green, fruity-flavored olive oil)

200 grams potatoes, cleaned and thinly sliced

100 grams leeks, cleaned and thinly sliced

5 grams maple syrup, plus more to taste

Kosher salt

50 grams Italian parsley, picked

Zest of 1 orange

Tangerine oil

1. In a heavy-bottomed pan, bring the sake to a boil over medium heat. Set 12 mussels aside and add the rest to the pot. Cover the pot with a lid. When the mussels have opened, remove the pot from the heat and strain the liquid through a cone filter. Remove the mussels from their shells and place them back in the strained cooking liquid. Set aside.

2. Place the water chestnuts in a small hotel pan and cover them with Chinese black vinegar. Compress in a vacuum chamber two or three times until translucent. Reserve until needed.

3. In a sauté pan, heat 100 grams of the olive oil over medium-low heat. Add the potatoes and leeks and sweat until tender but not colored, about 10 minutes. Transfer the potato mixture and the mussel mixture to a blender and purée until smooth. If it's too thick, thin it with water. Emulsify with the remaining 325 grams of olive oil. Add the maple syrup and season with salt.

4. In a small saucepan, bring a couple tablespoons of sake to a boil. Add the remaining 12 mussels, cover the pot with a lid, and steam until they open, about 3 minutes.

5. Reheat the soup and ladle it into 4 bowls. Press water chestnuts into the soup from the center out up to the rim. Place a mussel on top of each one, giving the effect of the mussels floating on the soup's surface. Garnish with parsley leaves, orange zest, and a drizzle of tangerine oil.

WHY SOUP?

Soup has always factored heavily into my menus. We had a lentil soup at Prime in Las Vegas that we had to pass through a chinois three times to get the right texture. We did it on New Year's Eve once, and my sous-chef, who later became the chef de cuisine, was like, *You're crazy, this is nuts. Make it stop.*

Every New Year's Eve he sends me a text: "Are you passing the soup three times?" He's haunted by it. But that much labor translates into a real difference.

UNI EGG DROP SOUP

During the first couple years of wd~50, we didn't want to use luxury ingredients—we wanted to figure out how to make familiar, more humble ingredients *feel* luxurious. But I'd be lying if I said I didn't get excited about high-end ingredients, and that's what happened here.

The uni egg drop soup was a collaboration with sous-chef J.J. Basil. I thought, *Egg drop soup . . . uni is an egg, can't you just swap uni for egg?* And then J.J. was tasked with figuring out how to do it.

His method was anything but foolproof; one could easily screw it up. Eggs are so volatile, the temperature had to be exactly right, and the curds had to be just the right size. J.J. was the perfect person to make this dish, because he's the kind of guy who could sit there, focused on getting the swirl of the uni egg drop just right, while all hell was breaking loose during service. When it was right, it was a spectacular dish.

NOTE: *Do not place your fingers or any unsterilized utensils into the soup, as the enzyme amylase is present almost everywhere in a kitchen and will destroy the thickening properties of the starch.*

SERVES 8

600 grams Uni Drop Soup (page 108), chilled
Baby bok choy
Steeped Greens (page 109)

Thinly sliced radishes
Fried Oyster Mushrooms (page 109)
10 tongues uni

Into each bowl, ladle about 60 grams of cold uni drop soup. Garnish each bowl with two halves of baby bok choy, a few pieces each of the greens, radishes, and fried mushrooms, and 1 small tongue of uni. Serve immediately.

UNI DROP SOUP

Ginger Chicken Stock (recipe follows)

8 grams cold water

8 grams arrowroot starch

52 grams uni, at room temperature

120 grams egg whites, at room temperature

4 grams good-quality soy sauce, at room
   temperature

2 grams distilled white vinegar

1. In a large stockpot, bring the stock to a boil. Mean-while, make a slurry: Whisk the cold water and arrowroot starch thoroughly. Set aside.

2. After you've made the slurry, make the egg mixture: Use an immersion blender to blend the uni until smooth. Carefully mix the egg whites and uni with a fork until the mixture is thick and ropey. If you whisk too aggressively, the egg whites will break down, and you'll get a grainy, much-smaller drop. Do not completely homogenize the mixture—it should be more chunky than smooth. If you place a fork in the mixture and lift it out, there should still be some resistance on the eggs' part to pass through the slots of the fork. Set aside.

3. While whisking quickly, stream the slurry into the stock. Bring the mixture back to a boil, then sim-mer for 5 minutes to cook out the starch flavor. Turn off the heat.

4. Stir the soy sauce and vinegar into the egg mixture, then pour it into the stockpot in a clockwise direc-tion. With a whisk, gently keep moving the stock in a clockwise direction. When you see the egg clouds forming, place a lid on the pot. Let sit for 2 minutes.

5. With a ladle, gently transfer the egg clouds to a container. Place in an ice bath to cool. Reserve the broth.

GINGER CHICKEN STOCK

25 grams fresh ginger, peeled

1 kilogram chicken stock

65 grams soy sauce

45 grams distilled white vinegar

3.5 grams sugar

3 grams kosher salt

60 grams bok choy, cut in half

5 grams thinly sliced red radishes

1. Cut the ginger into ⅛-inch planks and crush them with the back of your knife.

2. Warm the chicken stock over medium heat until it's above room temperature—it should be liquid rather than congealed. In a container, combine the ginger and the chicken stock. Whisk for 1 minute. Cover and refrigerate overnight.

3. In a medium pot, combine the stock and ginger with soy sauce, vinegar, sugar, and salt. Bring to a boil. Reduce to a simmer, cover, and cook for 15 minutes, then remove from the heat. (If you're making the stock in advance, this is when you should chill it.)

4. Heat a cast-iron skillet or plancha until it's ripping hot. Cook the bok choy, turning as needed, until charred. Place in the stockpot and cover. Let steep for 10 minutes.

5. Place the radishes in the stockpot. Steep for an-other 5 minutes. Strain, then pass through a paper cone filter. Use that day, or the flavor will turn murky.

STEEPED GREENS

10 hearts baby bok choy

200 grams leafy greens, such as mustard greens or lamb's-quarters

20 grams good-quality soy sauce

2 grams rice vinegar

2 grams sugar

1. Bring a large pot of water to a boil. One at a time, blanch the bok choy and greens until tender but still crunchy, 5 and 2 minutes, respectively. Shock in ice water, then pat dry.
2. In a large bowl, combine the soy sauce, vinegar, sugar, and 200 grams of water. Place the greens and bok choy in the mixture and let steep at room temperature for at least 2 hours.

FRIED OYSTER MUSHROOMS

30 grams clarified butter

1 head oyster mushroom, torn into small, wispy pieces

Kosher salt

In a steel sauté pan, heat the butter over high heat. Fry the mushrooms until crispy, about 10 minutes. Pat down on paper towels and season with salt. Set aside until ready to use.

FROG LEGS, ROOIBOS CONSOMMÉ, SMOKED BRIOCHE, NASTURTIUM

The frog leg soup started as a joke between me and Ryan Henderson, the other Henderson, who was chef de cuisine at Alder. We thought it would be funny if we could do a dish with both frog and nasturtium, because nasturtium looks like a lily pad. I think we were drunk when we came up with the idea, but in the sober morning it still seemed like a viable path to a delicious dish.

Ryan decided to serve frog dumplings with roasted-carrot consommé and nasturtium at Alder. For my dish at wd~50, I wanted to fry the frog legs because, as a Southerner, I want to fry everything. Tea consommé seemed like the perfect, lightly astringent foil to the fried frog. And brioche purée, a nod to the idea of tea and brioche for breakfast, added a peanut-buttery richness, which, along with mushrooms, grounded the dish.

Techniquewise, the consommé was the most interesting element. There's a reason you don't see frog consommé very often: It's hard to make. Our first version was pretty terrible. It was just frog, and we cooked it for too long, so it tasted bitter and musty. Dion, a longtime prep cook, and I worked on figuring it out. We tried every which way, blanching the frogs once, blanching them twice. Ultimately we ended up blanching the carcasses twice, and then bringing them up a third time and cooking them for a half hour. A touch of soy sauce at the end rounded it out perfectly.

—Sam Henderson

SERVES 6 TO 8

Pickled Leeks (page 113)

Steamed Oyster Mushrooms (page 113)

Frog Leg and Rooibos Consommé (page 113)

Brioche Purée (page 114)

12 to 16 Fried Frog Legs (page 114)

6 to 8 small pieces nasturtium leaves

1. Warm the pickled leeks and mushrooms under a salamander. Bring the consommé to just under a boil.

2. On the lip of each soup bowl, place a swipe of brioche purée and lay 5 pieces of mushroom over the top. Twist 1 piece of leek at the incisions so it straddles the mushroom. Place a frog leg at the top and bottom of the purée and ladle about 1½ ounces of consommé into the bowl. Garnish with a nasturtium leaf.

PICKLED LEEKS

1 leek, white part only
100 grams verjus
100 grams red wine vinegar
100 grams beet juice
25 grams sugar
Kosher salt

1. Clean the leek bulb, then cut in half lengthwise. Cut each piece into planks about 2 inches long. Stacking the planks, cut three horizontal "teeth" by making two incisions about ¾ inch from either end, but stopping short of cutting through the plank. This will allow you to twist the leek on the plate. Set aside.
2. In a medium saucepan, combine the verjus, vinegar, beet juice, sugar, and 2 grams of salt and heat over medium heat, stirring so the sugar and salt dissolve. Set aside and let cool to room temperature.
3. Bring a medium pot of salted water to a boil. Blanch the leeks until tender, 2 to 3 minutes. Shock in the room-temperature pickling liquid. Vacuum-seal the cooled leeks and liquid in a cryovac bag. Refrigerate until ready to use.

STEAMED OYSTER MUSHROOMS

2 heads oyster mushrooms
Kosher salt
100 grams tamari
450 grams water

1. Pick the oyster mushrooms into petals, removing the roots.
2. Season lightly with salt and set in a perforated hotel pan or in the steamer insert for a pot or pan. In the bottom of the steamer, combine the tamari and water, bring to a boil, and steam the mushrooms over the mixture until tender but not soft, about 8 minutes. Cool and refrigerate until ready to use.

FROG LEG AND ROOIBOS CONSOMMÉ

We had delicious teas at wd~50 the whole time it was open. Rachael Carron, my dad's wife, is originally from Dublin and was in charge of the tea program, because it made sense to have an Irishwoman in charge of tea. I found it wonderfully ironic that she only ever served Japanese teas. We started messing around with cooking fish in tea, crusting things in tea. And then Sam came up with the idea of making a consommé out of it—and I thought that was really clever.

—Wylie Dufresne

This was an interesting thing to teach somebody else how to make, because a twenty-year-old kid who drinks Red Bull every day generally doesn't know much about rooibos tea. I tasted some versions where they'd throw the tea in at a rolling boil for much longer than it should have been in there, and it was just disgusting. Brewed properly, it's delicious.

—Sam Henderson

100 grams fresh ginger, sliced

20 small frog legs, with spines

2 bay leaves

2 medium onions, cut into 1-inch cubes

1 medium carrot, cut into 1-inch cubes

5 grams black peppercorns

2 heads garlic, halved

Rooibos tea leaves

Soy sauce

1. Heat a dry skillet or plancha over high heat. Add the ginger and cook until charred, 5 to 10 minutes. Set aside.
2. On to the frogs: Separate the thighs from the calves and spines. (Set aside the thighs—those are for the Fried Frogs Legs, right.)
3. Place the calves and spines in a small pot. Fill the pot with cold water just under the level of the bones, bring to a simmer, and drain. Repeat. Do this a third time, but this round, instead of draining, skim the stock and add the bay leaves, onions, carrot, black peppercorns, and garlic. Cook over low heat for 30 to 60 minutes; you are looking for a nice, subtle flavor, like a chicken stock but less forward. Once the flavor is there, add the toasted ginger, turn the heat off, and cover for 15 minutes. Strain. Measure the strained stock.
4. Bring the stock back to 180°F and add 15 grams of rooibos tea leaves per 375 grams of stock. Cover and steep for 3 minutes, then strain. (We then clarified the broth in a centrifuge, but you can also serve it as is.)
5. To serve, warm the consommé and season with soy sauce.

BRIOCHE PURÉE

75 grams cold butter, diced

200 grams Brioche (page 236), cubed

300 grams warm water

3 grams kosher salt, or to taste

1. Place the butter on a half hotel pan and place in a smoker. Fill another half hotel pan with ice and place below the pan of butter. Cold-smoke the butter one cycle, 10 to 15 minutes.
2. Place the brioche cubes in a single layer on a sheet pan. Toast under a salamander, or in a 400°F oven, until golden brown, 2 to 3 minutes.
3. In a blender, process the brioche on high to a coarse powder. While the blender is running, stream in the water, then add the salt. Throw the butter in one cube at a time to emulsify, working with a tamper—the paste will be thick at this point. Once the butter has been incorporated, remove the purée, pass through a tamis, and cool quickly over an ice bath to keep it from breaking.

FRIED FROG LEGS

12 to 16 frog thighs, reserved from Frog Leg and Rooibos Consommé (left)

Neutral oil, for deep-frying

Frog Brine (page 115)

Frog Dredge (page 115)

1. French the frog thighs by scraping the flesh down along the bone so it resembles a lollipop. Clean the exposed bones with a cloth or small paring knife.
2. In a medium pot, heat the oil to 375°F. Drop the frog thighs in the buttermilk brine, then into the dredging mixture. Tap lightly to remove excess coating. Deep-fry until light golden brown, about 2 minutes. Set aside on paper towels.

FROG BRINE

4 grams kosher salt

480 grams buttermilk

10 grams ground pink peppercorns

0.95 gram (0.2%) xanthan gum

In a blender, process the ingredients for 1 minute on medium speed. Refrigerate until ready to use. (Why xanthan in a brine? The brine doubles as part of the dredge and gives you a thicker coat.)

FROG DREDGE

225 grams Crisp Coat

10 grams ground pink peppercorns

5 grams kosher salt

25 grams rooibos tea leaves

In a large bowl, combine the ingredients, then sift through a coarse tamis. If the rooibos leaves get caught in the tamis, reincorporate them into the mixture.

FOIE
GRAS

From the moment wd~50 opened until we announced we were closing, some critics questioned our approach to food and our interest in manipulating it. I thought we were just doing what so many chefs before us had done: We were taking ingredients and saying, *How can we turn these into dinner?* Before we were making edible eggshells and fried mayonnaise, Frenchmen labored over elaborate galantines and ballotines; they broke down beasts (and for that matter, fruits and vegetables), pulled them apart, filled them with stuffing, and stitched them back together.

Manipulating food is not a new thing. Why are there so many shapes of pasta? We all know why: because bending food to your will and your whims reflects how you see the world—and because sometimes you end up with a better-tasting end product. You can cook a whole leg of lamb by just throwing it on the coals, but if you butterfly it, stuff it, tie it back up, and cook it slowly and evenly, you get something much more delicious.

There is no ingredient better suited to manipulation than foie gras. Yes, you can simply cut it and sear it. But taking it apart and reforming it is so much more compelling. You can turn it into terrines. You can liquefy it. You can make a mousse out of it. It's so versatile in the hands of people who appreciate it, respect it, and want to make the most of it. And it can show up in any part of the meal, from the beginning to the very end. This set of dishes is wd~50's contribution to the foie conversation.

FOIE GRAS AND ANCHOVY TERRINE, CITRUS CHUTNEY, TARRAGON

This was the first foie dish on the menu at wd~50, and like a few of our other early creations, it was polarizing. The diners who loved it really loved it; the ones who hated it really hated it. Blogger Steve Plotnicki said it was one of the worst dishes created in the history of man.

The dish wasn't meant to provoke. It started with a scribble in an old notebook: "foie gras and anchovy." Surf-and-turf is a combination that works across all cultures, so one of our cooks, Fran Derby, and I created this dish, starting with white anchovies and foie stacked on top of each other. We eventually landed on a version with a thin, shingled layer of anchovies on top of a rectangle of foie gras terrine. The richness of the foie and the briny acidity of the white anchovies didn't need much else, but we added citrus and cocoa nibs to round out the flavors and textures. Regardless of what Plotnicki said, I stand behind it.

SERVES 6

Citrus Chutney (page 122)

Fresh tarragon

Tarragon Sauce (page 122)

6 rectangles Foie Gras and Anchovy
  Terrine (page 122)

Maldon salt

Candied Cocoa Nibs (page 123)

On each plate, place a small quenelle of chutney. Garnish with a tarragon leaf. With a spoon, drag one line of tarragon sauce down the plate, from 1 o'clock to 7 o'clock. Place a rectangle of the terrine next to it and season with Maldon salt. Finish the plate with 1 teaspoon of cocoa nibs cascading from the bottom corner of the terrine.

CITRUS CHUTNEY

12 grams grapefruit flesh, minced

12 grams orange flesh, minced

12 grams Pickled Golden Raisins (recipe follows), minced

6 grams lemon flesh, minced

6 grams lime flesh, minced

1.75 grams tangerine oil

10 leaves Italian parsley, chiffonaded

Kosher salt

In a large bowl, combine all of the ingredients and season with salt. Pour the mixture into a cheesecloth and hang for 30 minutes to drain excess liquid. Refrigerate until ready to use.

PICKLED GOLDEN RAISINS

50 grams golden raisins

5 grams yellow mustard seeds

50 grams Champagne vinegar

100 grams water

40 grams maple syrup

Place the raisins and mustard seeds in a heatproof container. In a saucepan, combine the vinegar, water, and maple syrup and bring to a boil. Cover the raisins with the boiling liquid, cool to room temperature, then refrigerate until ready to use.

TARRAGON SAUCE

1 egg

60 grams fresh tarragon leaves

125 grams water

200 grams grapeseed oil

Kosher salt

1. Poach the egg in a 147°F water bath for 2 hours. Cool in an ice bath immediately. Set aside.
2. Bring a small pot of water to a boil. Blanch the tarragon for 5 minutes. Shock in ice water, then squeeze out all the water. Roughly chop.
3. In a small blender (it's difficult to start the sauce in a large blender), blend the water and tarragon for at least 1 minute; the mixture should be well incorporated but not smooth, per se. With the motor running, add the egg, then slowly dribble in the oil until emulsified. Season with salt. Pass the purée through a chinois and place immediately in an ice bath.

FOIE GRAS AND ANCHOVY TERRINE

250 grams Prepared Foie Gras (page 124)

12 to 14 marinated anchovies (boquerones), depending on size

1. Line a small rectangular (4½ x 6-inch) tray or container with plastic wrap, making sure there are no wrinkles in the plastic.
2. Melt/temper the foie gras in a warm place or in 10-second bursts on low in the microwave until it is pourable. (If the mixture breaks, reemulsify it with an immersion blender.) Pour the foie into the lined tray to a height of about ⅓ inch. Refrigerate until firm.
3. Turn the pan over, pop out the foie, and remove the plastic. Temper for about 5 minutes, then with a

clean, sharp knife, cut 4 rectangles from the terrine. (The trick is cutting at just the right temperature: too cold and the foie will have crumbly, jagged edges; too warm and it will get mushy.) Keep the foie rectangles cold.

4. Lay 6 or 7 marinated anchovies on a cutting board, skin side down. They should be slightly overlapping, like Venetian blinds or shingles on a roof. Place 2 foie rectangles on top. Using a knife, trim the anchovies to fit the size of the foie, then flip the rectangles over. Press gently to adhere the anchovies to the foie. Repeat with the remaining foie and anchovies. Refrigerate until ready to use.

CANDIED COCOA NIBS

500 grams water, plus 20 grams more for deglazing
500 grams sugar
130 grams cocoa nibs
Neutral oil, for frying

1. In a small saucepan, combine the water and sugar and heat over medium heat, stirring, until the sugar dissolves.
2. Add the cocoa nibs to the simple syrup and bring to a boil. Boil until the syrup becomes viscous and molasses-like, 10 to 15 minutes. Deglaze with water and bring back to a boil.
3. Strain through a chinois, waiting for a moment to let all the syrup fall.
4. Heat a pot of oil to 375°F.
5. Scoop the nibs out of the chinois and then, using the same chinois, fry the nibs in small batches: Lower the chinois into the oil and fry until the nibs are crunchy, 1 to 2 minutes. Transfer to a silicone baking mat and let cool slightly. Blot on paper towels, then let cool completely. Store in a plastic container at room temperature until ready to serve.

PREPARED FOIE GRAS

When I worked at Jean-Georges Vongerichten's JoJo, and later at Jean-Georges, I cleaned hundreds and hundreds of pounds of foie gras. And the more I worked with it, the more I wondered whether I was telling the foie what to do, or vice versa. It was like working with clay: Is the clay saying, *Bring me this way*? Or am I saying, *I'm going to shape you that way*?

Removing the veins is an art. There are two veins: one bigger, one smaller. The process of finding the veins, pushing the liver away and gently pulling them out, is so tricky. I've seen cooks, myself included, turn the whole lobe into cottage cheese. There really isn't a diagram or rulebook for this process; it's organic matter, it changes. And it's a lot like butter: The more you handle it, the more it melts. You're moving this stuff around, trying to get every vein, and then suddenly it's melting everywhere, and the French boss walks by your station and says, *Oh la la! You ruined it! Don't tell anyone you worked here.*

Learning to clean foie gras happens only one way: by doing it over and over again. You'll mess some up along the way, but you can always turn it into a terrine.

2 lobes Grade A foie gras (1 to 1.4 kilograms)

Kosher salt

White pepper

10 to 14 grams Instacure #1 (1% of the weight of the liver)

45 grams Cognac

45 grams dry sake

1. Let the foie gras sit at room temperature for at least 2 hours. It should be soft before cleaning.
2. Remove the veins from the foie gras and discard. Lay the foie gras on top of a small tray seasoned with salt, pepper, and half the Instacure.
3. In a small bowl, combine the Cognac, sake, and the remaining Instacure. Pour over the foie gras. Sprinkle with salt and pepper. Cover with plastic and let sit for 1 hour. Remove the plastic and drain.
4. Heat the oven to 200°F.
5. Place the foie gras on a half-sheet pan and put it in the oven. Remove when it is warm and soft to the touch or when it reaches an internal temperature of 104°F, about 5 minutes. Check with a meat thermometer or thermocouple, or look for a bit of fat to have rendered and the lobe to give a little with a gentle tap. Remove the foie from the oven and pass it through a tamis. If it breaks or separates, reemulsify it with a whisk or immersion blender in a bowl set over ice.
6. Transfer the passed foie into plastic containers and refrigerate until ready to use.

FOIE GRAS, CANDIED OLIVES, GREEN PEAS, BEET JUICE

This was the second iteration of our liquid-center foie gras, one that Mike Sheerin and I created: We replaced nori with beet juice, which would ooze blood red all over the plate when diners cut into the terrine. The combination of flavors—salty olives, pea soil for crunch, and vegetal sweetness—was unexpected, but it worked.

SERVES 6

Pea Soil (page 128)
6 Foie Gras Cylinders with Liquid Centers
   (page 128)

Maldon salt
16 pieces bull's blood greens
24 pieces Candied Black Olives (page 129)

1. Place a spoonful of pea soil off center on each plate. In the palm of your hand, clasp the circumference of a foie mold, as though you were warming a pat of butter. Do this for 15 to 20 seconds. Then take the plastic off. Place your index and middle fingers along an invisible line that runs the diameter of the mold. Push and gently pop the foie out onto the soil.

2. Season the foie gras with Maldon salt, then garnish with 4 pieces of bull's blood greens and 4 pieces of candied olives. Instruct guests to cut into the foie right away.

PEA SOIL

Pea soil was one of many savory streusels we made to put familiar flavors on the plate in unexpected ways. This one was bright green and paired nicely with the beets and olives.

> 250 grams almond flour
> 250 grams sugar
> 100 grams freeze-dried peas, blitzed
> 2 grams kosher salt
> 300 grams butter, melted

1. Sift together the almond flour, sugar, pea powder, and salt. Add the melted butter, and mix well. Pack into a small pan lined with plastic wrap. Let cool.
2. Heat the oven to 180°F.
3. With a box grater, grate the mixture onto a parchment-lined sheet pan and spread into an even layer. Bake until dry and crumbly, 8 to 10 minutes. Hold at room temperature until ready to serve.

FOIE GRAS CYLINDERS WITH LIQUID CENTERS

> 250 grams Prepared Foie Gras (page 124)
> 4 frozen Beet-Olive Centers (recipe follows)

1. Prepare four 2 x 1.5-inch ring molds: Cut 3-inch squares of plastic wrap and wrap them tightly around the bottoms of the molds. Arrange the molds on a sheet pan or tray.
2. Melt/temper the foie gras in a warm place or in 10-second bursts on low in the microwave until it is pourable. (If the mixture breaks, reemulsify it with an immersion blender.)
3. Place a pastry bag or gallon-size resealable plastic bag over a quart container or large cup and fill with the foie. Check the viscosity of the foie: Before

piping, the foie should behave like pudding. If it's thick like peanut butter, it's too cool; if it's fluid like heavy cream, it's too warm. Chill in the fridge or temper until it's just right. This is crucial to filling the ring molds and supporting the caramel in the center of the cylinder as the foie cools.

4. Snip a ¼-inch opening with a pair of scissors. Pipe the foie into the ring molds, stopping when they are three-fourths full. Nestle a frozen beet plug into the center of the mold—it is important to center these dead-on in the foie cylinder. Top with more foie gras to cover, lift up the mold, and tap a few times on the tray. Level the top and refrigerate until the foie is firm like chilled butter, at least a couple of hours and up to 1 day.

BEET-OLIVE CENTERS

500 grams beet juice
80 grams kalamansi lime juice
60 grams dextrose powder
2 egg whites
75 grams Kalamata olives, pitted and rinsed
Xanthan gum
Kosher salt

1. In a small saucepan, combine the beet juice, lime juice, and dextrose and bring to 140°F.
2. In a blender, process the egg whites with the olives. Whisk into the beet mixture and bring to a gentle simmer. Allow the egg whites to coagulate and poke a hole in the middle of the raft. Start skimming the juice through this hole over the egg raft. Cook until the juice looks clean of solids, 5 to 10 minutes, skimming the top as necessary. Using a ladle, gently strain the mixture through a chinois.
3. Weigh the liquid and measure 0.4% of the total weight in xanthan gum. Shear the xanthan gum into the clarified juice, then season with salt. Cool over an ice bath.

4. Pour the juice into ¾-inch-diameter plastic sleeves and freeze. Once frozen, slice crosswise into disks about ⅜ inch thick and keep frozen until needed.

CANDIED BLACK OLIVES

100 grams Kalamata olives, pitted and rinsed
350 grams simple syrup
25 grams water
Neutral oil, for deep-frying

1. Halve the olives crosswise, then cut each half into quarters. Place in a dehydrator overnight.
2. In a saucepan, combine the olives and simple syrup and bring to a boil over medium heat. Boil until the syrup becomes viscous and molasses-like, 10 to 15 minutes. Deglaze with water and bring back to a boil. Strain through a chinois and wait for a moment to let all the syrup fall.
3. Heat a pot of oil to 375°F.
4. In small batches, fry the olives until crispy and glassy, 2 to 4 minutes. Remove to a silicone baking mat, taking care to separate the olives as they cool. Store at room temperature until ready to serve.

KNOT FOIE

I always thought that tying food into a knot would be impressive, at least from a presentation standpoint. I tried egg yolks first: I cooked them in a thin tube long enough so I could tie them into a knot, but eating the end result was like biting into a pencil eraser.

I might have given up on the knot idea except that we came across some information about gums that would eventually lead to knotted foie gras. We learned that xanthan gum and konjac gum, when combined, make a gel that's superelastic. Of course, we knew from working with gums, or hydrocolloids, that they couldn't be used to gel fat. The name "hydrocolloid" says it all: You need water to hydrate the gum. So we had to figure out the least amount of water we could add to our foie gras to hydrate the gums without affecting the texture and flavor of the terrine. In the end we added a bit of agar as well, so we could handle the foie gras over and over again and manipulate it into a knot without melting it.

For the finished dish we wanted to balance hot, sweet, and sour. We added heat and acidity in the form of kimchi (bought at the Union Square Greenmarket); the sweetness came from amazing Iranian golden raisins. The final touch was crunch, from Japanese puffed rice balls.

SERVES 8

Foie for Knots (page 132)

50 grams arare (Japanese puffed rice balls)

Kimchi Purée (page 132)

Golden Raisin Purée (page 132)

Maldon salt

Delfino cilantro sprigs

1. Slice the foie lengthwise into strips about ⅜ inch wide.

2. Tie each strip into a knot and place on a plate. Top the knot with rice balls. Dot both the foie knot and the plate with the kimchi and raisin purées. Season with Maldon salt. Garnish with a few sprigs of delfino.

FOIE FOR KNOTS

450 grams Prepared Foie Gras (page 124)

150 grams water

2.1 grams konjac gum

1.2 grams agar

0.9 gram xanthan gum

1 egg yolk

1. Put the foie and the water in separate containers and place them in the microwave. Melt the foie until its temperature reaches 180°F (it will separate) and the water is between 120° and 130°F. Though power varies from microwave to microwave, we typically put both the foie and the water in on medium for 1 minute, then on high for 30 seconds. Then we removed the water and finished the foie on high for another 15 to 30 seconds.
2. Using an immersion blender, shear the konjac, agar, and xanthan gum into the foie. With the same immersion blender, blend the egg yolk into the water. Slowly drizzle the yolk-water mixture into the foie gras mixture, blending vigorously as you go; you want an emulsified mixture. Pour the mixture immediately into a shallow baking tray, roughly 9 x 13 inches. Tap the tray on the counter to remove any air. Let cool for 2 hours.

KIMCHI PURÉE

250 grams prepared cabbage kimchi

0.5 gram xanthan gum

Blend the kimchi until smooth. Add the xanthan gum and blend for 30 seconds more. Place in a squeeze bottle. Refrigerate until ready to use. Be aware that your squeeze bottle may become possessed and bubble over if left too long at room temperature—kimchi is, after all, a fermented product!

GOLDEN RAISIN PURÉE

200 grams Iranian golden raisins

300 grams hot water

4 grams xanthan gum

Kosher salt

1. In a small bowl, steep the raisins in the water until tender and plumped, about 30 minutes. Drain.
2. In a blender, process the raisins until smooth. Add the xanthan gum and purée for 30 seconds more. Season lightly with salt and place in a squeeze bottle. Refrigerate until ready to use.

BUSTED FOIE: FOIE GRAS, FENNEL, MALT, SHERRY VINEGAR JAM

Liquid nitrogen has been a bit overhyped. It looks super cool and it photographs well, but it really only does one thing: freezes the bejesus out of whatever it touches. This can be useful for grinding things (liquid nitrogen will instantly make almost any ingredient brittle), but the coolest use we found for it at wd~50 was our busted foie.

Foie gras never looks brittle or sharp because it is almost entirely fat, and fat doesn't naturally form right angles. We were excited about freezing foie gras with nitrogen because we could then shatter it into rough-looking shards that you never would have guessed were foie gras.

SERVES 4

"Busted" Foie Gras (page 136)

Vinegar Jam (page 136)

100 grams baby fennel, thinly sliced and
    dressed with olive oil

24 Malt Puffs (page 136)

12 pieces celery sprouts

15 grams amber malt powder

On each plate, scatter the frozen foie in a broad arc. Place 3 or 4 piles of vinegar jam around the foie and cover with slices of fennel. Place 6 malt puffs intermittently around the plate. Scatter 3 celery sprouts on top and dust with malt powder.

"BUSTED" FOIE GRAS

240 grams Prepared Foie Gras (page 124)
2 liters liquid nitrogen

1. Slice the foie into roughly ½-inch-thick planks.
2. Place the sliced foie into a deep metal container and pour half of the liquid nitrogen onto it. Once frozen solid, transfer the foie to another container. Smash the foie, adding nitrogen as needed, until it resembles small pieces of broken rock or rubble. A pestle works well for this.
3. Store in the freezer until ready to serve. This is best to do day-of, or the foie will oxidize.

VINEGAR JAM

250 grams sherry vinegar
275 grams sugar
6 grams pectin
50 grams glucose syrup
4 grams citric acid

1. In a medium saucepan, bring the vinegar to a boil. Whisk in 25 grams of the sugar and the pectin, then return to a boil.
2. Add the glucose and the remaining 250 grams of sugar. Bring the mixture to 223°F. Whisk in the citric acid and pour directly onto a plastic tray to cool.
3. In a stand mixer fitted with the paddle attachment, beat the cooled mixture until you get a jamlike consistency, about 2 minutes. Place in a pastry bag with a small tip. Refrigerate until ready to use.

MALT PUFFS

100 grams soy milk
1 gram iota carrageenan
1 gram Versawhip
0.2 gram calcium lactate
10 grams brown sugar
2 grams amber malt powder
0.2 gram kosher salt

1. In a medium saucepan, heat the soy milk to a simmer. Transfer to a blender.
2. Shear in the carrageenan for 1 minute. Add the Versawhip and shear for 1 minute. Add the calcium lactate, brown sugar, malt powder, and salt and shear for 1 minute more. Cool over an ice bath.
3. Using a hand mixer, whip the mixture to stiff peaks. Transfer to a pastry bag fitted with a ⅓-inch piping tip.
4. Pipe the mixture onto a sheet of acetate into dime-size hemispheres. Dehydrate overnight at around 145°F. The final puffs should keep their hemisphere shape and have the crunchy texture of astronaut ice cream.

AERATED FOIE

I found the tool that helped us render this exceptionally light and airy version of foie gras in an unlikely place: late-night QVC. The FoodSaver is a plastic box with a one-way valve and a hose on its lid, designed so you can remove air from the box and keep the fruits and vegetables inside fresher. We had something different in mind: We put our standard prepared foie gras inside the box, then we put that box inside a larger vacuum chamber (the one we used for cryovacing and sealing foods for sous vide cooking). When we turned the vacuum on, it pulled air out of the FoodSaver box and forced the foie gras to rise like a soufflé. It was as light and airy as an angel food cake, and it melted in your mouth.

With the help of lecithin (in the form of an egg yolk), some agar, and konjac, we tricked the air into staying inside of it. We rounded out the dish with simple accompaniments: beets, brioche, and plums.

SERVES 6

Aerated Foie (page 140)

Sour Plum Sauce (page 141)

18 plugs Roasted Beets (page 141)

18 pieces Toasted Brioche (page 141)

Maldon salt

Delfino cilantro leaves

Tear the aerated foie into 18 pieces (about the size of small plums). Place 3 of these pieces on each plate. Sauce the plate with 3 dots of sour plum sauce and garnish with 3 plugs of roasted beet. Arrange several pieces of brioche around the foie gras, season with Maldon salt, and finish with delfino leaves.

AERATED FOIE

This preparation is incredibly sensitive to temperature and agitation after aeration. We "practiced" with butter many times before moving on to foie gras so as not to waste a ton of money learning how to finesse it.

This recipe is scaled to aerate within a FoodSaver container that measures 12.8 x 7 x 6 inches (a capacity of 5.8 quarts). Dry the container completely and place a piece of tape firmly over the valve on the lid of the container. You will also need a vacuum chamber large enough to hold the FoodSaver container, and a small weight to place on top: 2 pounds is adequate.

316 grams Prepared Foie Gras (page 124)

100 grams water

1.6 grams no-boil agar

1 sheet silver sheet gelatin, bloomed in ice water

1 egg yolk

1. Melt the foie gras in the microwave on medium power until it reaches 120° to 130°F.
2. Bring the water to 180°F in the microwave. With an immersion blender, shear in the agar, then the gelatin, then the egg yolk. With the blender running, slowly trickle in the foie gras, blending until emulsified.
3. Transfer the mixture to a bowl and cool to between 82° and 85°F by continuing to mix the solution with the immersion blender. This will begin to aerate the foie. Wipe down the sides of the bowl with a spatula periodically.
4. Pour the mixture into the FoodSaver container, cover with the lid, place in the vacuum chamber with the weight on top, and turn the machine on. Once the foie rises to the top, stop the vacuum.
5. Ever so gently remove the container from the machine and place in the freezer. After 10 minutes, move the foie to the refrigerator. Chill for an additional 2 hours before serving.

SOUR PLUM SAUCE

Sour Iranian plums plus sweet beet juice plus savory miso—this sauce is a good example of our approach to building flavors and trying to find a way for bitter, sweet, salty, sour, and umami to come together in a single preparation.

300 grams dried Iranian sour plums, pitted

100 grams water

75 grams beet juice

25 grams red miso

25 grams sugar

1 gram xanthan gum

Rehydrate the plums in the water. Transfer the plums and soaking liquid to a blender. Add the beet juice, miso, and sugar and purée until smooth. Add the xanthan gum and blend again. Refrigerate until ready to use.

ROASTED BEETS

450 grams kosher salt

4 medium red beets

1. Heat the oven to 400°F.
2. Pour a bed of kosher salt into a small roasting pan and place the beets on top. Cover with foil and roast until a knife slides through the center of a beet with little resistance, about 1 hour. Let cool, then peel with a dry towel.
3. Portion into small plugs with ring cutters about ⅔ inch in diameter. Refrigerate until ready to use.

TOASTED BRIOCHE

165 grams Brioche (page 236), crusts removed

Kosher salt

1. Heat a convection oven to 200°F.
2. Shave the broad side of the brioche paper-thin on a deli slicer, trying to keep the slices intact. Cut each slice into roughly 2-inch lengths.
3. Crumple foil into uneven shapes, enough to cover a half-sheet pan. (A tuile mold may also be used.) Lay the bread over the top of the foil, season with salt, and bake until crisp, about 10 minutes. Break into organic shapes. Hold at room temperature until ready to use.

NOODLES

MISO SOUP, INSTANT TOFU NOODLES

This miso soup dish was born out of my brief obsession with methylcellulose. Methylcellulose is a hydrocolloid, or a gum—agar, gelatin, and carrageenan are all in the family. Most gums are temperature-dependent: You boil a liquid, the gum dissolves and becomes suspended in the liquid (this is called hydration), and when the mixture cools, the gum causes the liquid to set. It's like Jell-O: You dissolve a packet in hot water, and it sets in the refrigerator. Most gums gel upon cooling, but because God has a sense of humor, there happens to be one gum—methylcellulose—that gels when it gets hot. Think about how cool this is: You can take water mixed with methylcellulose, heat it in the microwave, and it'll come out solid. When I learned this I thought, *There must be a million things we can do with this.* And we started with tofu noodles.

When we developed this dish, I realized that we could have some fun with it at the table. The soup itself was a very traditional miso soup that we clarified. The noodles, though, showed off methylcellulose in all its glory: To replace the cubes of tofu that would typically be in miso soup, we puréed tofu with a little water, toasted sesame oil, and methylcellulose, and we put that into individual squeeze bottles for each customer. We'd bring the soup to the table with the squeeze bottle, and when people squirted the liquid (which was the consistency of heavy cream) into the hot soup, the liquid set and turned into noodles.

SERVES 6

Olive oil

4 shiitake mushroom caps, sliced

1 scallion, greens thinly sliced on the bias and held in ice water

600 grams Miso Soup (page 148)

Instant Tofu Noodles (page 148)

1. In a sauté pan, heat a slick of olive oil over medium heat. Sauté the shiitake mushrooms until cooked through, about 5 minutes. Set aside.

2. Divide the shiitakes and scallion among 4 warmed soup bowls. Ladle 100 grams of soup into each bowl and serve each with a squeeze bottle of the tofu mixture. Direct guests to squeeze the tofu into the soup and stir. Tofu noodles will form instantly.

MISO SOUP

1 kilogram Dashi (page 51), warmed to 120°F

10 grams red miso paste

4 grams (0.4%) silver sheet gelatin, bloomed in ice water

1. In a saucepan, warm the dashi to 120°F. Whisk in the miso paste. Whisk the gelatin into the soup. Let cool to room temperature, then freeze.
2. Thaw the soup in the refrigerator in a sieve lined with cheesecloth. Harvest the clarified miso soup and rewarm before serving.

INSTANT TOFU NOODLES

100 grams water

4 grams methylcellulose (A16M)

225 grams medium-firm tofu

Kosher salt

Toasted sesame oil

1. In a small saucepan, bring the water to a boil over high heat. Shear in the methylcellulose. Transfer the mixture to a blender, add the tofu, and process until smooth. Season to taste with salt and sesame oil. Cool down to 55°F in an ice bath.
2. Place the mixture in a pastry bag and pipe into small individual squeeze bottles, around 44 grams in each. Make sure the bottles are completely full or the diner may have trouble dispensing the tofu. Refrigerate until ready to serve.

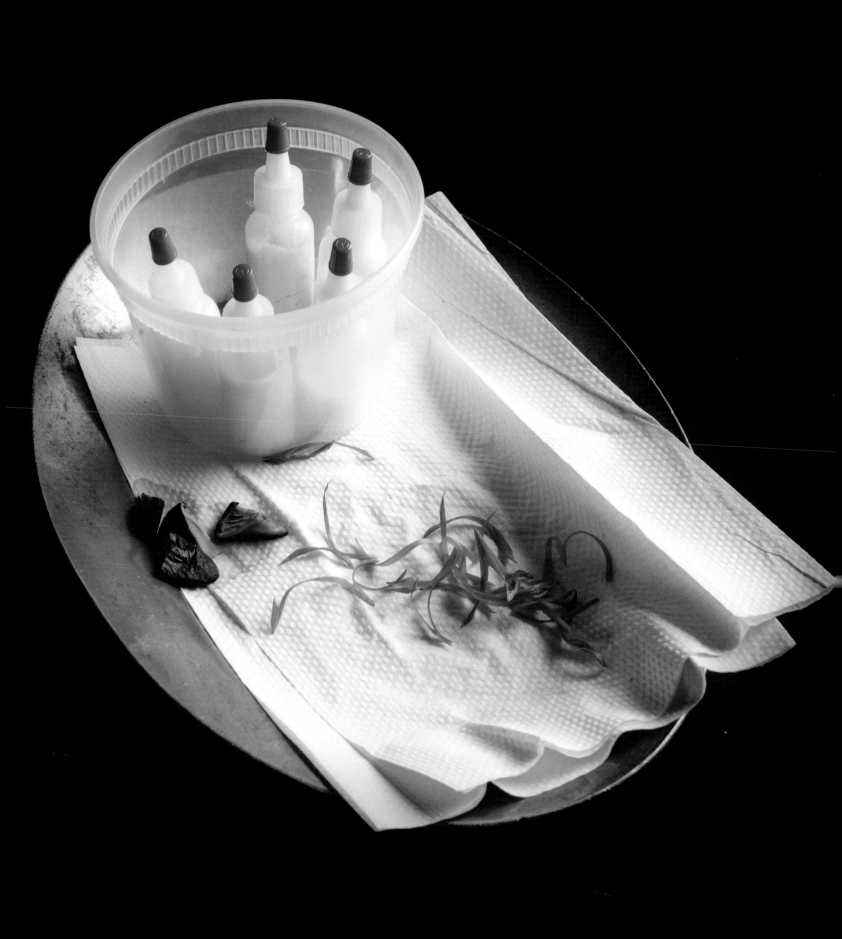

SCALLOPS, PINE NEEDLE UDON, GRAPEFRUIT DASHI, CHINESE BROCCOLI

Ramen is the crowd-pleaser noodle and soba is the connoisseur's favorite, but I've always had a soft spot for udon, a thicker, chewier Japanese noodle. The traditional method for kneading udon is to stomp on the dough. And while there are many classic techniques we chose to move past at wd~50, this was one we kept: We'd cryovac it and stomp the daylights out of it.

The finished dish looks like a typical bowl of Asian noodles, but that familiarity evaporates with the first taste of grapefruit-spiked dashi and pine-scented noodles.

SERVES 6

4 stalks Chinese broccoli

Kosher salt

Clarified butter

12 Scallops (page 153)

20 grams butter

6 portions Pine Needle Udon (page 153)

4 red radishes, thinly sliced

800 grams Grapefruit Dashi (page 153)

Pine Oil (page 153)

1. Put a large pot of water on to boil for the udon.

2. Thinly slice the Chinese broccoli stems and chiffonade the leaves. Steam the stems until tender, 2 to 5 minutes. Season with salt and set aside.

3. Heat a sauté pan over high heat. Add clarified butter and sear the scallops on one side until golden brown. Add the whole butter and baste the scallops until cooked through.

4. Boil the udon for 3 minutes. Drain and divide among the serving bowls.

5. Top the noodles with the scallops, Chinese broccoli stems and leaves, and sliced radishes. Divide the dashi among the bowls, then drizzle with a few drops of pine oil. Serve immediately.

A properly seared scallop is one of my all-time favorite pieces of seafood. The texture is unlike anything else that comes out of the ocean. When I was young, I loved putting scallops into a hot pan and searing them like a steak; the Maillard reaction is just as effective on scallops as it is on a piece of meat. The center would end up warm but still raw, and the outside would be crisp and brown.

At wd~50, I backed away from that intense searing method. We started by brining them, which kept them plump and juicy, then we gently cooked them in a low-temperature water bath. Once they were cooked through, I could sear them just enough to bring out the sweetness without putting a thick, chewy quarter inch of browned skin on the outside.

Remember, when you're searing scallops—or anything, really—you must pat them dry. If they're wet, or if you salt them too early and the salt brings moisture to the surface, the water comes in contact with the oil and pushes it away from the surface of the protein, causing the scallops to stick to the pan.

Pans made of cast iron or blue steel are the ideal cooking vessels for scallops, because they get really hot. And clarified butter is the ideal fat: It has a high smoke point and big flavor. Olive oil also has a high smoke point, but not as high as clarified butter, and when the oil reaches its smoke point, its flavor changes in a way I don't like.

You'll want to put the pan over the heat dry. Do *not* add the fat yet; you can get the pan so much hotter dry than you can once the fat is in it. Once the pan is really hot, take it off the heat, add the butter (a good ounce, for a shallow-fry), and lay the dry scallops in the pan. Don't overcrowd them. All of this stovetop cooking happens in about 2 minutes. Remember, the scallops have already been cooked through in the water bath, so you're just giving the surface some texture. You're looking for a much lighter color than the scallops you might have made in the past. When one side is golden, I tell the cooks to flip the scallops, wait a couple seconds, then take them out of the pan. If they're done right, they'll be creamy and white on the inside, and lightly caramelized on the outside.

SCALLOPS

18 medium scallops

Kosher salt

Cayenne pepper

Season the scallops with salt and cayenne and divide them between two vacuum-sealed cryovac bags. Cook sous vide in a 122°F water bath for 12 minutes. Remove and allow the scallops to rest in their bags.

PINE NEEDLE UDON

100 grams water

12 grams kosher salt

5 drops pine oil

250 grams bread flour, plus more for dusting

1. In a medium bowl, combine the water, salt, and oil. Set aside.
2. Place the flour in a food processor. Drizzle in the liquid, pulsing to incorporate. Transfer the mass to a large bowl and bring together into a ball. Place the dough in a large, sealable bag and knead it on the floor with your feet, folding it over itself 10 times (this is the most effective method, and the traditional method, for handling a dough this firm). It should feel tough. Let the dough rest for at least 3 hours or up to overnight.
3. Roll the dough through a pasta machine to about ⅛ inch thick, then cut it into noodles about ⅛ inch wide. Portion into 60-gram piles and arrange them on a flour-dusted sheet pan. Wrap in plastic wrap and freeze until ready to use, up to 1 week.

GRAPEFRUIT DASHI

945 grams Dashi (page 51)

1.25 kilograms grapefruit juice

Grated zest of 1 grapefruit

4.25 grams (0.2%) agar

Soy sauce

1. In a large bowl, combine the dashi, grapefruit juice, and grapefruit zest.
2. Blend 1 cup of the dashi-grapefruit mixture with the agar and pour into a saucepan. Place over high heat and bring to a boil. Simmer for 5 minutes to hydrate the agar.
3. Meanwhile, bring the remaining dashi-grapefruit mixture to 140°F.
4. Combine the two mixtures, then pour into a shallow pan. Let cool completely; the mixture will firm up.
5. Using a whisk, break the mixture into curds and place in a cheesecloth-lined chinois. Let sit for 1 hour at room temperature; the resulting liquid should be clear. Season with soy sauce and set aside. Reheat gently before serving.

PINE OIL

200 grams spruce shoots (these are available in the spring)

300 grams grapeseed oil

1. In a blender, process the spruce shoots and oil on high for 2 minutes. Let cool to room temperature.
2. Vacuum-seal the oil in a cryovac bag and cook sous vide in a 158°F water bath for 1 hour. Cool in an ice bath. Discard the solids.

CHICKEN LIVER SPAETZLE, PINE NEEDLE, RADISH, COCOA NIB

We went crazy with spaetzle at wd~50—we tried making them out of everything. But before we experimented, we turned to Kurt Gutenbrunner, New York's greatest Austrian chef, for the quintessential recipe. He's the Jedi Master of the form, and he makes his spaetzle with quark, a thick sour cream. I started messing with that formula, substituting other ingredients for the quark. One of the most difficult versions of spaetzle we created was made with Worcestershire. We couldn't add straight Worcestershire because we needed to use too much liquid. We tried reducing the Worcestershire to intensify it, but that was disgusting. Eventually, we figured out that we could add xanthan gum to thicken the Worcestershire to the right consistency.

For this variation, we drew inspiration from the size and shape of spaetzle and enlisted meat glue to make spaetzle out of chicken liver.

SERVES 6

8 grams clarified butter

Chicken Liver Spaetzle (page 156)

Butter

5 grams Shallot Confit (page 50)

10 pieces Pickled Bean Sprouts (page 156)

Kosher salt

Pine Emulsion (page 156)

Candied Cocoa Nibs (page 123)

4 red breakfast radishes, shaved on a mandoline

Olive oil

Maldon salt

Pea shoots (optional)

1. Heat a sauté pan on medium-high heat. Add the clarified butter and two large spoonfuls of spaetzle. Sear until browned, then add a pat of whole butter, the shallot confit, and the pickled bean sprouts. Toss a few times to warm through. Check the seasoning and add salt if needed.

2. Brush the perimeter of a bowl with the pine emulsion and sprinkle cocoa nibs all around. Plate the spaetzle mixture, top with the radishes, and sprinkle with olive oil, Maldon salt, and pea shoots, if using. Serve immediately.

CHICKEN LIVER SPAETZLE

280 grams skinless chicken thigh meat, cut into a large dice

280 grams chicken livers, cleaned and soaked overnight in milk

65 grams chicken skin

9 grams (1.5%) Activa RM

5.5 grams (0.75%) Instacure #1

3 grams kosher salt

1. Lay the thigh meat, livers, and skin on a few sheet pans and parfreeze. Pass through a meat grinder 3 times using the smallest die.
2. Place a stand mixer bowl and paddle in the freezer for 10 minutes.
3. In the cold bowl, combine the chicken-liver mixture, Activa RM, Instacure, and salt and beat at medium speed until homogenized, about 3 minutes.
4. Place the farce in a half hotel pan and compress twice in a vacuum chamber (hit start, then stop before the mixture boils over). This removes air from the farce. Let sit for at least 30 minutes.
5. Bring a large stockpot of water to a gentle simmer, roughly 180° to 200°F. Place a perforated hotel pan over the top and press the farce through the holes in small batches using a bench knife. Hold the scraper perpendicular to the perforated pan to produce nice, short spaetzle.
6. Once the spaetzle float, pull them from the pot using a spider and shock in an ice bath. Remove as soon as they're cooled and store in a plastic container. Refrigerate until ready to serve.

PICKLED BEAN SPROUTS

150 grams cleaned and trimmed mung bean sprouts

200 grams distilled white vinegar

300 grams water

100 grams sugar

5 grams kosher salt

Place the mung bean sprouts in a heatproof bowl or other vessel. In a saucepan, bring the vinegar, water, sugar, and salt to a boil and pour over the sprouts. Cool and let sit in the refrigerator for 24 hours before serving.

PINE EMULSION

2 egg yolks

1 lemon, juiced

300 grams grapeseed oil

15 grams parsley juice (for color!)

3 drops spruce essence

Kosher salt

Place the egg yolks and lemon juice in a food processor. With the machine running, add 1 tablespoon of the oil at a time. Once you see it start to catch, continue adding the rest in a slow, steady stream. Add the parsley juice and spruce essence and pulse 4 or 5 more times. Season with salt to taste. Refrigerate until ready to use.

CUTTLEFISH, CARROT, CHAMOMILE, SCHMALTZ

At its root, this is surf and turf, a combo that is inexplicably popular the world over. The base of the dish is cuttlefish, which is like squid's cousin—it has much thicker flesh, but it's equally briny and delicious.

We used medium cuttlefish, a little smaller than a Frisbee. Once we cleaned out the inner armor (cuttlefish have a plate inside that you need to remove), we cooked it sous vide, low and slow, and then charred it—hard. There was an auditory cue that it was being done right: The steam escaping through the flesh would make an eerie whistling sound.

After we'd cooked, charred, and chilled the fish and sliced it into noodles, we'd add all the extras: carrot sauce, dried chamomile flowers, and schmaltz. Schmaltz, or chicken fat, is one of the less celebrated but most delicious of animal fats. Back at Jean-Georges, we'd scoop two or three inches of clear, flavorful fat from the top of our chicken stock and use it in place of butter or olive oil for frying potatoes or eggs, or sautéing a piece of fish. For this dish we set the chicken fat with gellan before freezing and grating it so it wouldn't dissolve right away when eaten—it lingers for a moment before it melts.

SERVES 4 TO 6

Marinated Carrots (page 160)
Cuttlefish Noodles (page 160)
10 grams lemon juice
Carrot Sauce (page 160)

Chicken Fat (page 161)
Dried chamomile, ground
About 20 pea shoots (and pea blossoms when available)

1. Heat the carrots and cuttlefish noodles until just warmed through.

2. Dress the cuttlefish with the lemon juice.

3. Sauce the interior walls of each bowl with the carrot sauce in a circular, orbital manner. Lay 40 to 50 grams of cuttlefish noodles and 3 to 4 pieces of carrot in the lap of each bowl. Using a Microplane, finely grate some chicken fat over each bowl. Dust with dried chamomile and garnish with pea shoots.

MARINATED CARROTS

50 grams cumin seeds

75 grams coriander seeds

2 cinnamon sticks

1 dried chipotle or Costeño pepper

750 grams grapeseed oil

Kosher salt

2 bunches baby carrots of all colors, peeled and scrubbed (small, tender carrots, not those whittled things from the bags at the supermarket)

1. In a dry medium saucepan, toast the cumin, coriander, cinnamon, and chipotle over medium heat until fragrant, about 2 minutes. Pour in the oil and reduce the heat to low. Infuse, covered, for 3 hours.
2. Blend the oil mixture on high for 4 to 5 minutes. Let cool.
3. Separate the oil mixture in a centrifuge, strain through a paper cone filter, and discard the solids. (If you don't have a centrifuge, you can let the oil settle overnight, then siphon through a chinois and through a paper cone filter, but the whole time you'll be asking yourself, *Why don't I own a centrifuge?*)
4. Bring a large pot of salted water to a boil. Blanch the carrots until tender, 7 to 8 minutes. Shock in the oil and let cool to room temperature. Portion into thumb-size pieces cut on the bias.

CUTTLEFISH NOODLES

1.2 kilograms cuttlefish tails

30 grams olive oil

Kosher salt

1. Using a dry towel, clean the cuttlefish of its membrane. Dress with the olive oil and season with salt. Vacuum-seal in a cryovac bag. Cook sous vide in a 131°F water bath for 16 minutes.
2. Heat a cast-iron or blue steel pan until ripping hot. (If you have a flattop range, you can place the fish directly on the eye, no pan.) Sear the cuttlefish, pressing down aggressively with towels (or something to insulate your hand from the sputtering heat of the pan) to get an even char. (The cuttlefish should make a screeching sound if you apply proper pressure.) Freeze, then shave into broad noodles on a deli slicer around setting #2. Reserve.

CARROT SAUCE

600 grams carrot juice

30 grams rice vinegar

0.92 gram (0.4%) xanthan gum

4.5 grams kosher salt, or more to taste

In a small saucepan, cook the carrot juice over the lowest heat possible until reduced by two-thirds (to 200 milliliters). (Depending on the heat source, this could take anywhere from 1 to 3 hours.) Blend the carrot juice, vinegar, and xanthan gum until smooth and season with the salt. Refrigerate until ready to use.

CHICKEN FAT

200 grams chicken fat (preferably skimmed off
   chilled chicken stock)

2 grams dried chamomile

0.5 gram white pepper

305 grams water

0.3 gram sodium citrate

10 grams low-acyl gellan gum

1.25 grams iota carrageenan

5 grams kosher salt

0.5 gram calcium lactate

1 egg yolk

1. In a large saucepan, combine the chicken fat and
   chamomile. Let steep over low heat for 1 hour. Season with the white pepper.

2. Strain the fat through a chinois into a clean saucepan. Bring to 210° to 225°F over medium heat.

3. In a separate saucepan, bring the water to a boil.
   Transfer to a blender and shear in the citrate, then
   the gellan, then the carrageenan. With the motor
   running, drizzle in the fat to emulsify the mixture.
   Add the salt, calcium lactate, and egg yolk and
   blend to combine. Pour the mixture into a plastic
   pint container and let cool. Hold in the refrigerator
   until ready to use.

POACHED DIVER SCALLOP, BERBERE GRANOLA, CARROT-MARCONA RAVIOLI, DASHI

By using meat glue and gelatin together, we found we could create noodles out of pretty much anything. In this recipe, we used sheets of carrot to create ravioli with a smoky Marcona almond filling; in the next, we made lobster noodles and tossed them with grapes, charred lemon bits, and picked lobster meat.

SERVES 6

Carrot-Marcona Ravioli (page 164)

Dashi-Lime Sauce (page 165)

Berbere Granola (page 166)

8 to 12 pieces Poached Scallops (page 166)

Berbere Oil (page 166)

Sea salt

Pea shoots

1. Heat the ravioli until just warmed through (we put them in a CVap oven at 131°F for about 6 minutes), then flash under a salamander.

2. For each serving, spoon dashi-lime sauce into the center of a wide bowl. Sprinkle a spoonful of granola on top, and place a ravioli on top of the granola. Flank the ravioli with 2 or 3 pieces of scallop on either end, twisting the two edges of the scallop in opposite directions before turning onto the plate. Garnish with berbere oil, sea salt, and pea shoots.

CARROT-MARCONA RAVIOLI

> 6 rectangles Smoked Marcona Gel (page 165)
> 6 Carrot Sheets (recipe follows)

For each ravioli, lay a piece of almond gel in the center of a carrot sheet. Fold the wrapper over the gel lengthwise, then fold the other ends over tightly, like a gift. Trim any excess wrapper. Refrigerate until ready to use.

CARROT SHEETS

> 250 grams Carrot Purée (recipe follows)
> 50 grams water
> 5 grams Activa TI
> 12.5 grams silver sheet gelatin, bloomed in ice water
> Cooking spray

1. In a saucepan or in the microwave, bring the carrot purée to 98°F.
2. Split the water between two vessels: 25 grams in a bowl, 25 grams in a small saucepan. Whisk the Activa into the water in the bowl. Bring the water in the saucepan to 160°F, and whisk in the gelatin to dissolve. Combine the slurries.
3. Place the carrot purée in a blender and shear in the slurry. Place in a small pan, then inside a vacuum chamber. Compress 2 or 3 times, stopping the cycle before the purée boils over. This will remove the air from the carrot mixture.
4. Wipe a countertop with a damp towel. Lay a sheet of plastic down and wipe it with a dry towel so that it adheres to the counter without wrinkles. Place a few spoonfuls of the purée down on the plastic and lay another piece of plastic over the top. Using a rolling pin, gently roll the purée between

the plastic to the thickness of about 2 sheets of paper. Stretch tightly and lay on a sheet pan between 2 sheets of acetate to keep them from getting wrinkled. Repeat until all of the purée has been used. Let set in the refrigerator for at least 4 hours.

5. Peel the plastic wrap off the carrot sheets and transfer them to a cutting board. Cut carrot sheets to 2¾ x 3½ inches. Place between sheets of parchment that have been coated with cooking spray. Refrigerate until ready to use.

CARROT PURÉE

24 grams brown sugar

20 grams Dijon mustard

2 tablespoons water

20 grams thinly sliced shallots

2 grams garlic, sliced

3 grams berbere spice

340 grams carrots, scrubbed and peeled

0.7 gram (0.2%) xanthan gum

Kosher salt

1. In a wide sauté pan, dissolve the brown sugar and mustard in the water over low heat. Add the shallots, garlic, and berbere and sweat until soft, about 5 minutes.

2. Add the carrots and cover with water by about 1½ inches. Cover the pan and steam until tender, about 15 minutes. Drain, reserving the liquid.

3. Measure 300 grams of the solids and 35 grams of the liquid and place both in a blender. Add the xanthan gum and blend again. Pass through a tamis and season with salt. Refrigerate until ready to use.

SMOKED MARCONA GEL

450 grams carrot juice

6 grams silver sheet gelatin

105 grams Smoked Marcona Almonds (page 40)

50 grams water

0.625 gram (0.2%) xanthan gum

1. In a small saucepan, reduce the carrot juice over the lowest heat possible by two-thirds, to 150 grams. (Depending on the heat source, this could take anywhere from 1 to 3 hours.)

2. Bloom the gelatin in ice water.

3. In a blender, process the carrot reduction, almonds, and water for at least 3 minutes. (This amount of time is necessary—the heat will dissolve the gelatin, and the aeration will create the proper texture.) Shear in the gelatin for 1 minute, then the xanthan gum. Pass the mixture through a chinois.

4. In a small, shallow pan, spread the mixture into a thin layer about ⅜ inch deep. Let cool over an ice bath until stiff.

5. Cut the almond gel into four ¾ x 1-inch rectangles. Refrigerate until ready to use. (Any remaining gel can be melted down and reused.)

DASHI-LIME SAUCE

100 grams Dashi (page 51)

4 grams dry sake

2 grams soy sauce

1.25 grams Persian dried lime powder

4.5 grams (4.5%) Ultra-Sperse 3

In a medium bowl, whisk the dashi, sake, soy sauce, lime powder, and Ultra-Sperse 3 until a thick sauce forms. Set aside.

BERBERE GRANOLA

150 grams rice flakes

100 grams Marcona almonds, finely chopped

20 grams brown sugar

2 grams kosher salt

20 grams maple syrup

20 grams grapeseed oil

2 grams berbere spice

15 grams candied ginger, diced

1. Heat the oven to 275°F. Line a sheet pan with a silicone baking mat.
2. In a large bowl, combine the rice flakes, almonds, brown sugar, and salt. Mix well.
3. In another bowl, mix the maple syrup and oil. Pour into the dry ingredients and mix well.
4. Spread the mixture onto the sheet pan and bake until crispy, about 1 hour, turning the pan halfway through.
5. Sift the berbere spice through a sieve over the granola. Let cool, then toss with the candied ginger.

POACHED SCALLOPS

1 kilogram water

60 grams kosher salt, plus more to taste

6 U-10 scallops, adductor muscles removed

Almond oil

5 grams Preserved Lemon (page 50), diced

1. In a large container or bowl, combine the water, salt, and scallops and brine for 5 minutes.
2. Drain the scallops, then dress with the almond oil and vacuum-seal in a cryovac bag. Cook sous vide in a 125°F water bath for 14 minutes.
3. Make an incision through the radius of each scallop, then slice the scallops into coins, about ⅛ inch thick, and toss with the lemon confit. Season with salt. Refrigerate until ready to use.

BERBERE OIL

25 grams berbere spice

100 grams grapeseed oil

Blend the berbere and oil on high for 4 to 5 minutes. Pour into a squeeze bottle.

LOBSTER ROE NOODLES, CHARRED LEMON, GREEN GRAPE, CORIANDER BROWN BUTTER CRUMBS

SERVES 6

Zest of 1 lemon, peeled into strips

Lobster Meat (page 170)

180 grams Lobster Roe Noodles (page 170)

1 stalk celery, sliced lengthwise with a mandoline as thinly as possible and held in ice water

12 green grapes, quartered

Lobster Dressing (page 171)

24 to 30 pieces Pickled Red Onion (page 171)

50 grams Coriander Brown Butter Crumbs (page 171)

1. Heat a flattop or cast-iron skillet until ripping hot. Char the lemon zest on all sides. Let cool, then brunoise.

2. In a large bowl, toss the lobster meat, lobster roe noodles, celery, lemon zest, and grapes with the lobster dressing.

3. Place a large spoonful of the lobster mixture in the center of each bowl. Circle with 4 or 5 pieces of pickled onion and top with coriander brown butter crumbs.

LOBSTER MEAT

455 grams fresh seaweed (wakame or arame)

455 grams lobster claw meat

455 grams lobster knuckle meat

1. Place the seaweed in a large stockpot and cover with water. Bring to a boil, then remove the seaweed. Add the lobster meat and blanch until just cooked through, 3 to 4 minutes. Shock in ice water and pat dry.
2. Cut the meat into a medium dice. Save 150 grams of the not-so-nice pieces for Lobster Dressing (page 171).

LOBSTER ROE NOODLES

180 grams lobster roe

100 grams egg yolks

30 grams glycerin

1.8 grams kosher salt

1.25 grams (45%) xanthan gum

0.7 gram Activa RM

4.8 grams Ultra-Sperse M

1. In a blender, process the lobster roe, egg yolks, glycerin, salt, xanthan gum, and Activa until smooth. Pass through a tamis into a bowl. Whisk in the Ultra-Sperse.
2. Wipe a countertop with a damp towel. Lay a sheet of plastic down and wipe it with a dry towel so it adheres to the counter without wrinkles. Place a few spoonfuls of the purée down on the plastic and lay another piece of plastic over the top. Using a rolling pin, roll the purée between the plastic to the thickness of about two sheets of paper. Stretch tightly and lay on a sheet pan between two sheets of acetate to prevent wrinkling. Refrigerate while you repeat with the remaining purée.

3. Cook the sheets in a CVap oven at 194°F for 10 minutes. The lobster roe will turn a bright shade of orange when cooked. Let cool.
4. Transfer the sheets to a cutting board and slice into long, fettucine-like strips. Refrigerate until ready to use.

LOBSTER DRESSING

100 grams green grapes

100 grams clam stock

0.87 gram (0.25%) xanthan gum

150 grams lobster scraps (reserved from Lobster Meat, page 170)

In a small blender, process the grapes and stock into a coarse mixture. Rain in the xanthan gum, then add the lobster scraps. Blend until you get a smoothish, slightly coarse mixture, speckled through with tiny but discernible pieces of lobster and grapes. Refrigerate until ready to use.

PICKLED RED ONION

½ red onion, shaved on a deli slicer on setting #0.5

50 grams sugar

100 grams distilled white vinegar

200 grams water

In a saucepan, combine the onion, sugar, vinegar, and water and bring to a boil. Let cool. Vacuum-seal the onions and pickling liquid in a cryovac bag. Refrigerate until ready to use.

CORIANDER BROWN BUTTER CRUMBS

200 grams simple syrup

10 grams coriander seeds

10 grams water

Neutral oil, for frying

50 grams Brown Butter Solids (page 85)

1. In a saucepan, bring the syrup to a boil and add the coriander. Simmer on low for 30 minutes, or until the viscosity approaches that of molasses. Deglaze with the water. Return to a boil, then strain through a chinois.
2. Bring a pot of oil to 375°F. Using a small sieve, dip the coriander seeds into the hot oil for about 30 seconds. Let cool on a silicone baking mat.
3. Using a mallet or a small metal pot, crack the coriander seeds and combine them with the brown butter solids.

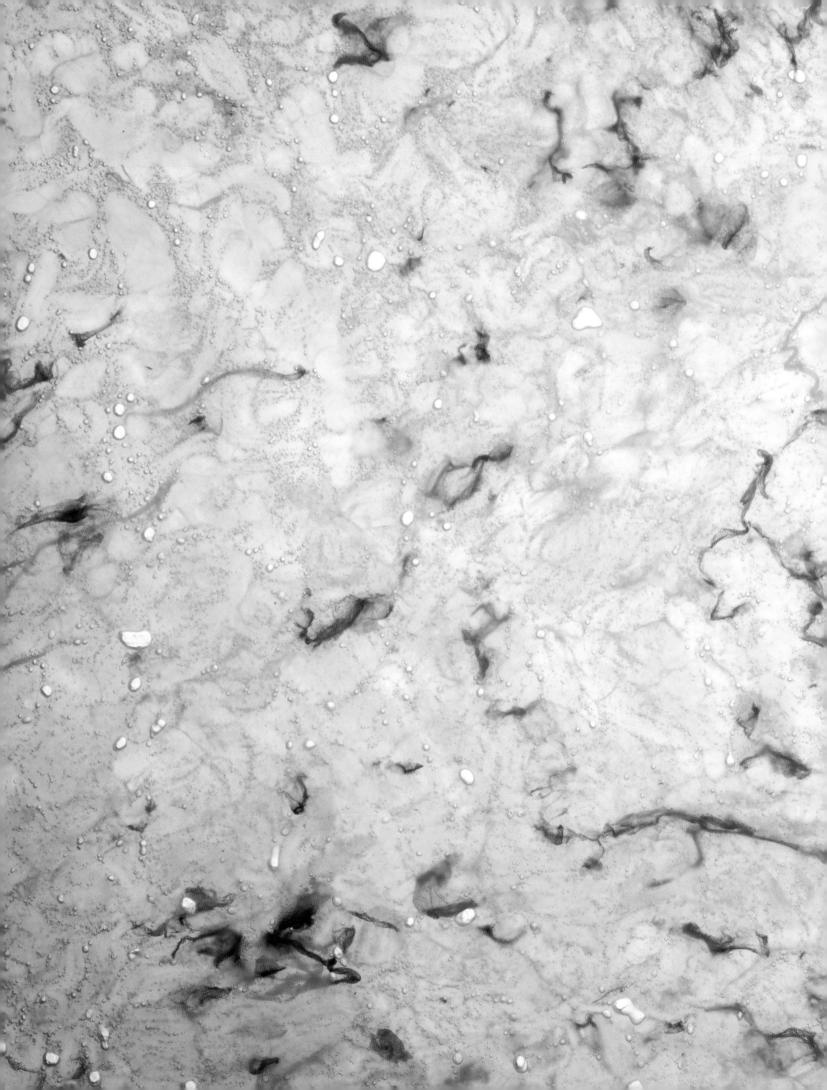

SHRIMP

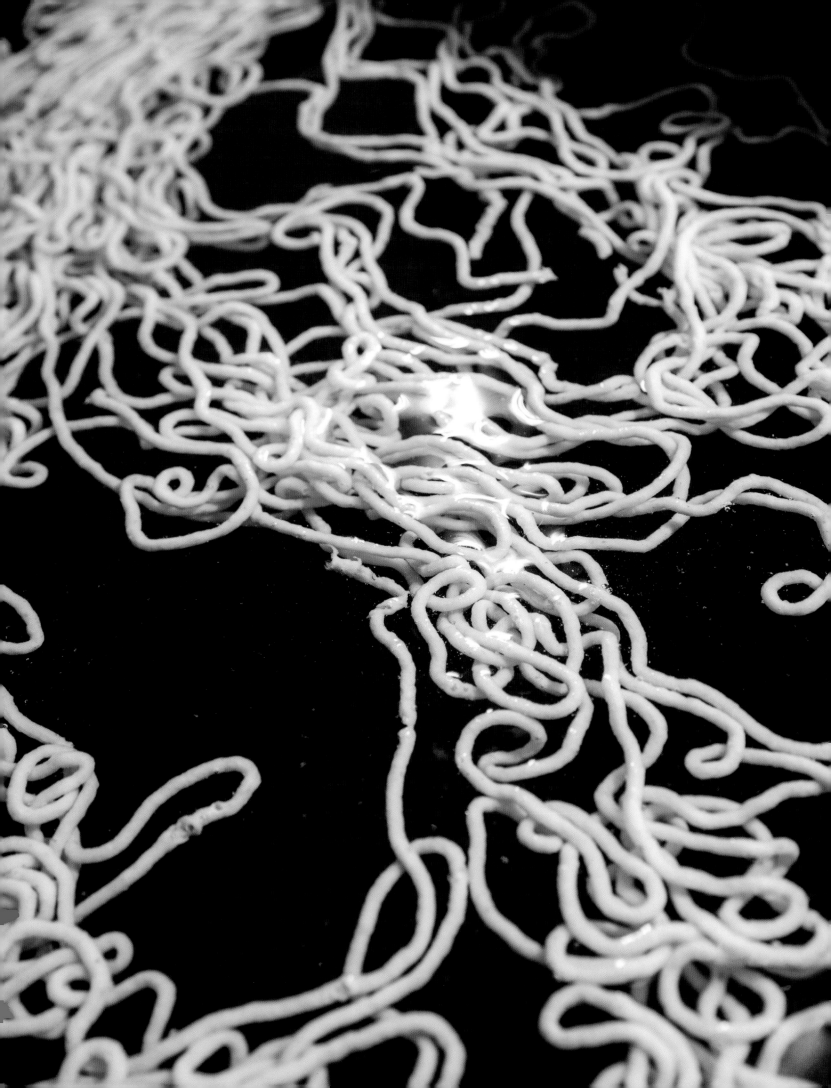

I was born in New England, and I spent a good part of my childhood consuming peel-and-eat shrimp. Even today, two or three times a month, I'll put a few pounds of frozen shrimp on a sheet pan with a little butter and pop them in the oven just until they're translucent, then the whole family will eat them until we're too stuffed for dinner.

I learned the fine art of cooking shrimp (or rather, barely cooking shrimp) from Jean-Georges. We'd put them on a sizzle platter with lots of butter, cook them under a salamander just until they curled, then pull them out and let the carryover heat finish them. When I was the chef at Prime in Vegas, we had a tank of live shrimp, and we served what I called "shrimp cocktail." We'd pull the shrimp out of the tank, cut them open, slather them in garlic butter, blast them in the salamander, and send them out. They were beyond delicious, and the people in Las Vegas *hated* them. They wanted cruise-ship shrimp cocktail.

Years later, at wd~50, we were able to experiment with shrimp in so many other ways, turning it into pasta, grits, and other unexpected forms.

SHRIMP NOODLES, SMOKED YOGURT, NORI POWDER

When this went on the menu at wd~50, we had already been using meat glue to stick pieces of protein together, but this was one of the first times we used the powder to fundamentally reshape a protein. It paved the way for many other types of "noodles."

The finished dish is shrimp-on-shrimp: noodles made of shrimp, garnished with Southeast Asian prawn crackers tossed in tomato powder. The yogurt adds tang and richness—and smoky notes. (Instead of just adding *pimentón,* or smoked paprika, to yogurt, we briefly cold-smoked the yogurt and added sweet Hungarian paprika.) To take the whole dish back out to sea, we finished it with dried, powdered nori.

SERVES 8 TO 10

Shrimp Noodles (page 178)
Shrimp Oil (page 179)
Water
15 grams butter

Smoked Yogurt (page 179)
Prawn Crackers (page 179)
Nori Powder (page 179)

1. In a small sauté pan, reheat the noodles over medium heat with a dash of shrimp oil, water, and the butter, stirring and tossing as needed.

2. For each serving, paint the yogurt onto a plate and top with a generous spoonful each of warm noodles and prawn crackers. Dust the plate with nori powder.

SHRIMP NOODLES

The formula for the noodles was pretty simple: shrimp puréed with salt, cayenne, and a dash of Activa RM (the type of meat glue we used in this and many other preparations). The method of turning that mixture into noodles was not so simple.

In the beginning, we were putting shrimp into a pastry bag with a pastry tip that had four holes. We'd pipe the purée onto parchment-lined sheet pans, pour warm water onto them (to cook the shrimp and activate the meat glue), then peel the noodles off and reserve them. Those were hard times.

Eventually Shea Gallante, who was then chef at Cru, gave me a tool to try—a Japanese pasta extruder. We set a circulating water bath to the temperature at which Activa RM is most active, then we squeezed the farce into the bath slowly with Shea's tool. The noodles were long, so we'd grab the spaghetti coil, pull out an appropriate length of noodle, and cut it with scissors. Snip, ice bath, repeat. We tossed the noodles with a little shrimp oil so they wouldn't stick together, and stored them for service.

250 grams peeled, deveined shrimp

0.5 gram Activa RM

3 grams kosher salt

0.15 gram cayenne pepper

Shrimp Oil (page 179)

Cooking spray

1. In a food processor, purée the shrimp, Activa, salt, and cayenne. Pass through a coarse tamis. Transfer the mixture to a pastry bag.
2. Set up a water bath to 136°F, but turn the motor off.
3. Pipe the mixture into a noodle maker, or extruder, and extrude all of the shrimp purée into the water bath. Cook for 2 minutes.
4. Using scissors, cut the noodles to the length of spaghetti and plunge them in an ice bath. Let cool.
5. Drain the noodles and separate them. Dress with shrimp oil and store on parchment paper lightly coated with cooking spray.

SHRIMP OIL

One day we realized we could boost the shrimp flavor in our noodles by adding a little shrimp oil to the farce. My oil is a classic Jean-Georges recipe—it's like making a stock but instead of adding water, you add oil. You brown your shells; add a little tomato paste, mirepoix, and tarragon; cook; and deglaze (the French like Cognac but we've used white wine, sweet wine, sake, white port). Once the booze has reduced, you cover it with grapeseed oil, heat it until it bubbles, then cool and steep it in the fridge overnight. The next day, you warm it back up and strain it, and you get this rich, flavorful oil the color of a dark rosé wine.

200 grams grapeseed oil
60 grams diced onion
60 grams diced carrot
60 grams diced celery
10 grams tomato paste
2 sprigs tarragon
60 grams white wine or dry sake
400 grams shrimp shells, chopped

1. In a large saucepan, heat about 1 tablespoon of the oil over medium heat. Add the onion, carrot, and celery and sweat until soft. Add the tomato paste, tarragon, and wine and cook, stirring, until the mirepoix is tender and the alcohol is cooked down, about 10 minutes. Add the shrimp shells and the remaining oil.
2. Bring the mixture to about 200°F and cover the pot. Remove from the heat and leave at room temperature for 3 hours, then refrigerate overnight.
3. The next day, reheat and strain the mixture through cheesecloth or a paper cone filter to harvest the shrimp oil.

SMOKED YOGURT

225 grams plain Greek yogurt
3 grams sweet paprika
Kosher salt

1. Spread the yogurt over a half hotel pan and place in a smoker above another half hotel pan filled with ice. Smoke the yogurt for 3 minutes.
2. In a medium bowl, combine the yogurt, paprika, and salt. Allow the flavors to infuse for 1 hour. Reserve.

PRAWN CRACKERS

This calls for uncooked prawn crackers, not the ones in the bag that are already puffed.

Neutral oil, for deep-frying
5 pieces prawn crackers
Tomato powder
Kosher salt

1. In a deep pot, heat 3 inches of oil to 375°F.
2. Crush a few prawn crackers with a mortar and pestle into irregular, smallish shapes. Deep-fry the cracker crumbs until they puff, about 1 minute. Pat down on paper towels, dust with tomato powder to coat, and sprinkle lightly with salt.

NORI POWDER

2 sheets sushi nori

Dry the nori sheets in a dehydrator set to 155°F for 3 hours or overnight in an oven with only the pilot light lit. Blend to a fine powder.

SHRIMP CANNELLONI, CHORIZO, THAI BASIL

Once we had shrimp noodles (page 178) figured out, we started considering other possibilities, like turning shrimp into a sheet to use for a filled pasta. With trial and error, we discovered that pounded shrimp was better than puréed for this application, both visually and texturally. We settled on cannelloni.

SERVES 6

4 Shrimp Cannelloni (page 182)

Butter

200 grams Chorizo Emulsion (page 182)

Olive oil

Maldon salt

30 pieces Thai basil flowers

1. Heat the oven to 140°F.

2. Remove the plastic from the shrimp cannelloni and cut them into thirds. Place them on a sheet pan that's been smeared with a thin film of butter and put it in the oven until warmed through, about 8 minutes. Flash under a salamander or broiler briefly.

3. On each plate, spread a broad, rectangular schmear of the chorizo emulsion with an offset spatula. Place 2 pieces of cut shrimp cannelloni on top. Garnish with a drop of olive oil, Maldon salt, and Thai basil flowers.

FROZEN SHRIMP ARE FINE

Shrimp freeze well, and frozen shrimp are often the best choice for home cooks, assuming you don't live right near a pier. The "fresh" shrimp in many supermarkets were likely frozen when they came off the boat and have simply been thawed by the folks in the seafood department.

SHRIMP CANNELLONI

SHRIMP FILLING
250 grams peeled, deveined shrimp, diced
25 grams Medjool dates, pitted and diced
4.25 grams Preserved Lemon (page 50), diced
1.5 grams Thai basil chiffonade
25 grams Pickled Bean Sprouts (page 156)
Kosher salt
Cayenne pepper

SHRIMP WRAPPERS
375 grams peeled, deveined shrimp, diced
3 grams kosher salt
0.15 gram cayenne pepper
1.5 grams (0.4%) Activa RM

ASSEMBLY
Thai basil

1. Make the shrimp filling: In a large bowl, combine the shrimp, dates, preserved lemon, Thai basil, bean sprouts, and salt and cayenne to taste. Cook a small amount of the filling on the stove to check the seasoning and adjust as needed. Refrigerate until ready to use.
2. Make the shrimp wrappers: In a small bowl, toss the shrimp with the salt, cayenne, and Activa.
3. Lay the mixture between 2 large sheets of plastic wrap and pound with a meat tenderizer until it is smooth and even. Using a rolling pin, roll out the mixture until you have a sheet that is slightly smaller than a half-sheet pan, about 12 x 12 inches. (If you have any extra, use the remaining mixture to make another sheet.) Let sit in the refrigerator, overnight or for a minimum of 4 hours.
4. Cook at 149°F for 3 minutes in a CVap oven. Shock by laying plastic over the top of the sheet pan and pouring ice on top of the plastic. Let cool.
5. Drain the sheet pan and peel off the plastic from both sides of the shrimp sheet. Pat the shrimp sheet gently with paper towels and portion into four 2¾ x 12-inch rectangles.
6. To assemble the cannelloni: Fill a pastry bag with the shrimp filling and snip about ½ inch off the tip with scissors. Lay a rectangle of plastic wrap down on the counter and place a shrimp wrapper on top of it.
7. Lay 6 to 8 medium leaves of Thai basil down the length of the wrapper, in the center. Pipe a line of shrimp filling on top of the Thai basil, then gently fold the edges of the wrapper up around it, using the plastic to guide it. We used a straightedge or ruler to tighten the cannelloni as we rolled them up.
8. Torque the cannelloni in the plastic wrap as you would a torchon and tie tightly on either end. Poke a few times with a cake tester to remove any air. Repeat for the remaining wrappers and filling, and refrigerate until ready to use.

CHORIZO EMULSION

1 egg
200 grams Spanish chorizo, removed from casing
160 grams water
130 grams grapeseed oil

1. Heat a circulating water bath to 147°F. Poach the egg in its shell for 45 minutes, then shock in ice water.
2. In a sauté pan, render the chorizo over low heat until cooked through, about 10 minutes. Transfer the chorizo to a blender, reserving the fat. Add the water and blend until smooth. Drizzle in the sausage fat, then the oil, blending until emulsified. Crack the egg into the blender and blend until the sauce lightens in color, about 20 seconds. Pass the mixture through a chinois and chill quickly.

SHRIMP COUSCOUS, AVOCADO, PAPAYA, CRISPY KAFFIR

Shrimp couscous started as scallop couscous, and scallop couscous started as an accident.

I don't remember what we were working on at the time, but one component consisted of diced scallops for a tartare. There was a good, young cook in the kitchen, Duncan, who completely overchopped them. I thought, *Accidents happen, no big deal, but I can't serve these raw because they're weird now.* So I put some butter in a pan, threw in the scallops, and, after a minute, the stuff looked like couscous, or at least Israeli couscous. I cooked the scallops until they sort of broke apart, cooled them down, pulsed them in a food processor—and then they *really* looked like couscous.

Scallop couscous went on the menu in a butternut squash soup seasoned with tamarind paste and garnished with a "lemon paper" made from lemon confit and egg whites. We slowly worked our way through the ocean with the couscous treatment: cod couscous was okay; squid couscous was intense, best in small doses. Shrimp was a big winner when we finally got to it.

Here we paired the couscous with two other big ideas from that time at wd~50: brûléed avocado and papaya "ravioli"—warm-climate neighbors brought together in a new way.

SERVES 6

24 pieces Papaya Ravioli (page 186)

Olive oil

Shrimp Couscous (page 186)

Avocado (page 186)

Kaffir Chips (page 187)

1. Heat the oven to 200°F. Place the papaya ravioli in the oven to warm through, about 3 minutes.

2. In a sauté pan, heat a slick of olive oil over medium-low heat. Add the shrimp couscous and cook, stirring, until warmed through.

3. On each plate, spread a schmear of the avocado mix with a small offset spatula. Using a blowtorch, brûlé half of the avocado mix—you can place a metal bench knife over the half you aren't torching to get a nice, clean line. Make a long mound of warm couscous running across and perpendicular to the avocado—two big spoonfuls should do it. Sprinkle with kaffir chips. Dot with 4 papaya ravioli. Drizzle with olive oil.

PAPAYA RAVIOLI

We were big on tropical fruit during the first three years of wd~50. Our pastry chef, Sam Mason, was a fan, plus the Latino grocery stores in our neighborhood stocked them. They were part of the Lower East Side *terroir*.

Back then we were also in the habit of dehydrating everything. Papaya and other fruits that are super high in sugar take forever to dehydrate. Dates, for example, get chewier and chewier as you dehydrate them but they don't ever crisp. With the papaya, we noticed that there was a point in the dehydration process when the pieces became like little ravioli—papaya skin around a juicy papaya center. The problem was that they could easily go past this stage and become a shriveled, one-dimensional fruit. So three times a night we had to put a batch in the dehydrator. They were a simple pleasure and a simple preparation, but not a mindless one.

250 grams very ripe but not too-ripe papaya, cut into 1-inch cubes

Place the papaya cubes in a dehydrator at 155°F until dry on the outside and juicy on the inside, 2 to 2½ hours. Set aside.

SHRIMP COUSCOUS

500 grams shrimp, peeled and deveined
40 grams butter
Kosher salt
Cayenne pepper

1. Pass the shrimp through a meat grinder using a fine die.
2. In a rondeau or large sauté pan, melt the butter over medium heat. Throw in the shrimp, season with salt and cayenne, and cook, stirring constantly, until cooked through, 6 to 8 minutes. Let cool completely.
3. Place the shrimp in a food processor and pulse until the mixture resembles couscous. Reserve.

AVOCADO

Torched avocado was in the wd~50 playbook for a long time. It came to us from AKA Café across the street, where the chef took an avocado and put sugar on it—a *lot* of sugar—and brûléed it. When he served it to me he told me everyone hated it, but I thought it was awesome. For this dish, we torched just half, to give it a charred flavor, and left the other half alone. Both sides played well with the papaya.

2 ripe avocados
75 grams Dijon mustard
75 grams plain Greek yogurt
50 grams olive oil
0.15 gram citric acid
Kosher salt

In a blender, process the avocados, mustard, yogurt, olive oil, and citric acid until very smooth. Season with salt to taste.

KAFFIR CHIPS

2 kaffir lime leaves
Olive oil
Kosher salt

1. Stretch plastic wrap tightly over a microwave-safe medium bowl and place the kaffir lime leaves on top. Sprinkle with olive oil and salt and cover with a second sheet of plastic. Poke several holes in the plastic and microwave for 2 minutes.
2. Place the layered plastic on paper towels and cool completely. The leaves will be crispy and can be broken into small pieces.

SHRIMP GRITS, PICKLED JALAPEÑO

During the life of wd~50, I always kept two notebooks: one for ideas, one for recipes. Taking these notes was important, but revisiting them was essential. I inevitably knew more when I returned to the ideas than I did when I came up with them.

One day, a few years after wd~50 opened, I wrote "shrimp grits" in my notebook, and it went in a pile of ideas that we never pursued. Many years later, I came across that note and thought, *I could make grits out of shrimp*—we knew how to make shrimp couscous so we could just make it even finer. I also figured I could add freeze-dried corn powder to make the shrimp grits taste appropriately corny. (Christina Tosi, the pastry chef who started Milk Bar, had played with corn powder when she worked with us, and years later used it to make Milk Bar's famous corn cookie.) Our resident Southerner, Sam Henderson, was from Atlanta and had a sense of what people from shrimp-and-grits country would expect out of the dish. She added the cryo-pickled jalapeño.

This dish was a strong part of our tasting menu from the day we started serving it, and it was a reminder of the importance of revisiting old ideas.

SERVES 6

2 scallions, greens only

Shrimp Grits (page 190)

Vegetable Stock (page 190; equal in
    weight to the shrimp grits)

100 grams freeze-dried corn powder

Kosher salt

60 grams butter

18 slices Pickled Jalapeño (page 190),
    each slice cut into quarters

1. Slice the scallion greens on the bias into 2-inch sections, then thinly slice those sections lengthwise and plunge them into a small bowl of ice water. Blot them dry and reserve for garnish.

2. In a medium saucepan, combine the shrimp grits, vegetable stock, and corn powder and whisk for 2 to 3 minutes over medium heat to thicken slightly. Season with salt to taste. Fold in the butter.

3. Spoon the shrimp grits into serving bowls and nestle a few pieces of the pickled jalapeños into each dish. Garnish with a few slivers of scallions.

SHRIMP GRITS

500 grams peeled, deveined shrimp

15 grams butter

Kosher salt

Cayenne pepper

1. Pass the shrimp through a meat grinder using a fine die and set aside. Clean and dry the grinder and its parts—you'll need it again later.
2. In a large sauté pan, heat the butter over medium heat. When it starts foaming, add the shrimp. Season with salt and cayenne and cook, stirring constantly, until cooked through, 8 to 10 minutes. The shrimp will clump together somewhat, but not to worry!
3. Grind the shrimp twice more, then place in a bowl over an ice bath. Let cool. Refrigerate until ready to use.

VEGETABLE STOCK

Reggie Soang, a sous chef, was developing this napa cabbage vegetable stock right around the time the shrimp grits came together, which is how the two ended up with each other. It's a simple but delicious all-purpose vegetable stock.

½ head napa cabbage, roughly chopped

1 small Spanish onion

2 cloves garlic

1 bay leaf

2 sprigs thyme

In a large stockpot, combine all of the ingredients and cover with water. Bring to a low simmer and cook, uncovered, for 45 minutes, skimming the surface as needed. Strain and let cool. Refrigerate until ready to use.

PICKLED JALAPEÑO

1 jalapeño, seeded and thinly sliced

25 grams sugar

3 grams kosher salt

50 grams distilled white vinegar

75 grams water

1. Place the jalapeño slices in a bowl. Combine the sugar and salt and sprinkle over the jalapeño. Let sit at room temperature for 10 minutes to "sweat." Rinse gently.
2. Vacuum-seal the jalapeño, vinegar, and water in a cryovac bag. Refrigerate until ready to use.

LANGOUSTINE, RED PEPPER, BLACK SESAME, SHISO

There's a lot of good technique in this dish—many textures and temperatures, and a balance of bitter, sweet, salty, sour, and umami. Sometimes you make dishes that you know are going to be crowd-pleasers, sometimes you make ones that are cook's dishes. This is a cook's dish.

On the plate, the shrimp stays in a recognizable shape, but we serve the red peppers as "Twizzlers." The Twizzlers were fluid gels, piped out and dehydrated to the right texture. I thought they'd play well with the sweetness and brininess of the shrimp or langoustines. To round out the dish we needed acid and herbs. We opted for a shiso oil and a bread sauce seasoned with black vinegar.

SERVES 6

6 langoustines

60 grams kosher salt

1 kilogram water

10 grams butter

Black Vinegar Sauce (page 194)

Red Pepper Pieces (page 194)

Red Pepper Strands (page 194)

Shiso Oil (page 194)

Micro shiso

1. Gently separate the head portion of the langoustines from the claws and the tails. Shell and devein them, remove their tails, and slice them in half.

2. Combine the salt and water in a large container. Brine the bodies of the langoustines for 3 minutes. Rinse and pat dry. Refrigerate until ready to use.

3. Smear a sizzle platter or sheet pan liberally with the butter and arrange the langoustines on it cut side up. Heat gently under the broiler until cooked through, 3 to 4 minutes.

4. Make a broad schmear of black vinegar sauce in the middle of each plate, and place a warmed langoustine on top. Arrange a few pieces of roasted pepper to one side of the langoustine. Using a fork, twist the red pepper strands into four nests and place one on each plate. Draw a few long lines of shiso oil on the plate. Garnish with micro shiso.

BLACK VINEGAR SAUCE

40 grams sourdough bread

50 grams Chinkiang black vinegar

50 grams water

100 grams olive oil

Kosher salt

1. Heat the oven to 200°F.
2. In a food processor, pulse the bread into crumb-size pieces. Lay the crumbs on a sheet pan in a single layer and bake until dry, 45 minutes to 1 hour.
3. In a blender, combine the sourdough crumbs, black vinegar, and water. With the motor running, slowly drizzle in the olive oil to emulsify. Season with salt to taste. Refrigerate until ready to use.

RED PEPPER PIECES

To make these, we roasted red peppers, peeled them, cut them into pieces, and then coated them in black sesame seeds, so they looked like blistered peppers. Flavorwise they make sense: Black sesame is a little bitter, a good foil for the sweetness of a bell pepper.

1 red bell pepper

50 grams black sesame seeds, crushed to a fine powder

1. Over an open flame, char the pepper until the skin turns black and can be removed easily. Remove the skin and seeds.
2. Cut the pepper flesh into 2 x ½-inch rectangles and dredge one side of each in the black sesame powder.

RED PEPPER STRANDS

These are like Twizzlers made from red bell peppers.

200 grams red bell pepper juice

2 grams low-acyl gellan gum

2 grams agar

Cooking spray

1. Pass the pepper juice through cheesecloth into a saucepan. Shear in the gellan gum and agar and bring to a boil. Cook for 5 minutes, then transfer to a small bowl set in an ice bath. Chill completely.
2. Blend the gel until smooth. Compress the mixture in a cryovac machine to remove any bubbles—do this in any open container, like a bowl—and repeat the process twice to ensure all the air is out of the emulsion.
3. Spray a couple of sheets of acetate cut to fit dehydrator trays with cooking spray, then wipe most of it off (the remaining slick is all you need). Place the red pepper purée in a pastry bag with a small tip and pipe directly onto the lined dehydrator trays. Dehydrate for 1 hour.

SHISO OIL

Kosher salt

100 grams shiso leaves

200 grams olive oil

1. Bring a small pot of salted water to a boil. Blanch the shiso until bright green, about 30 seconds. Shock in ice water and pat dry.
2. Pulse the shiso and olive oil together—we liked to keep this herb sauce a little chunky and rustic, not completely smooth. Season with salt.

FISH

ARCTIC CHAR, PURPLE BARLEY, SPICE BREAD, MUSHROOM JUS

When I worked at Prime, I realized that I could cook grains and beans in liquids other than water. I'd seen Jean-Georges juice anything and everything and use that in dishes where his French forebears would have used broth or stock. At wd~50, we tried cooking all sorts of grains in different juices, and the combination of barley and cabbage juice was striking. Barley intrigued me texturally (it was not something I ate as a kid) and when we combined it with cabbage juice, it was earthy, unexpected, and boldly purple.

To build a dish around this, we made our own pumpernickel bread, dehydrated it, crushed it a bit, and served that with salmon belly. We used albino king salmon in the early days. We'd score the flesh thoroughly—tiny, tiny scoring, back and forth—and then put the fish in the salamander for a minute or two, just until it started sizzling. The bottom of it would be on the warm side of raw, and the top would be crunchy. Eventually we moved to arctic char, a workhorse fish: It's deliciously fatty and easier to procure.

SERVES 6

Baby pea shoots

2 grams verjus

2 grams extra-virgin olive oil

200 grams Purple Barley (page 200), plus cabbage juice as needed

Arctic Char (page 200)

80 grams Pumpernickel Crumbs (page 200)

Mushroom Jus (page 200)

1. In a small bowl, toss the pea shoots with the verjus and olive oil.

2. In a small pot, warm the barley with a splash of cabbage juice over low heat, stirring frequently.

3. Score the fish and place under the salamander. When the flesh starts bubbling, it's ready.

4. Place 2 spoonfuls of barley on each plate and lay 1 piece of fish on top. Sprinkle a few pumpernickel crumbs next to the fish, garnish with pea shoots, and sauce with mushroom jus.

PURPLE BARLEY

205 grams pearl barley

710 grams red cabbage juice (from about
    2 cabbages)

Kosher salt

15 grams grapeseed oil

1. Place the barley in a dry pot over low heat. Toast as you would rice, stirring occasionally.
2. In a large stockpot, combine the barley, 500 grams of the cabbage juice, a big pinch of salt, and the grapeseed oil. Place over medium heat and bring to a slow simmer, skimming off the scum. Cover and cook over low heat until the barley is al dente, about 45 minutes. Stir and taste for seasoning. Add the remaining cabbage juice, stir, and let cool.

ARCTIC CHAR

1 kilogram water

60 grams kosher salt, plus more as needed

4 portions arctic char (110 grams each), trimmed, pin
    bones removed

Olive oil

1. Combine the water and salt in a bowl. Add the fish and brine for 5 minutes. Rinse.
2. Season the fish again with salt. Place in a resealable plastic bag with a drizzle of olive oil. Poach the fish in a 125°F water bath until medium-rare, about 10 minutes. To check, poke the fish with a cake tester; it should be warm to the touch when it comes out.

PUMPERNICKEL CRUMBS

80 grams pumpernickel bread, sliced

Dry the pumpernickel bread in a low oven or dehydrator until brittle. Crush into coarse crumbs. Hold at room temperature until ready to use.

MUSHROOM JUS

115 grams clarified butter

2.25 kilograms button mushrooms, cleaned and
    roughly chopped

2 heads garlic, broken into cloves

10 grams thyme sprigs

5 shallots, sliced

1 pinch kosher salt

120 grams water

475 grams chicken stock

Balsamic vinegar

Sherry vinegar

Walnut oil

1. In a roasting pan, heat the clarified butter over medium-high heat. Sweat the mushrooms until all their water has been released and they start to caramelize, about 10 minutes. Add the garlic, thyme, shallots, and salt and cook for about 2 minutes. Deglaze the pan with the water and chicken stock, scraping the fond from the bottom.
2. Transfer the mushroom mixture to a saucepan and barely cover with water. Simmer until the liquid is flavorful and the mushrooms are thoroughly cooked, about 1 hour. Strain through a chinois, then twist the solids through a kitchen towel to get all the liquid.
3. Return the liquid to the pot and reduce until it coats the back of a spoon, about 30 minutes. Taste, adding balsamic vinegar for sweetness and sherry vinegar for sharpness. Rewarm before serving, adding a splash of walnut oil.

CUTTLEFISH, BLACK GARLIC FEUILLETINE, FENNEL-LAMB FAT

Plating a dish like this is not easy—much like sushi, you have to work quickly so you don't spend too much time handling the fish. I told some of our cooks that the finished plate was supposed to look like the Sydney Opera House, but looking back I probably should have explained it in a simpler way.

The little fans of cuttlefish were nestled in dabs of lamb-fat purée—an idea that came from sous-chef J.J. Basil. J.J. did a lot of great work with purées at wd~50, and for this one, he mounted lamb fat into a fennel purée, which was super smart. Of all the animals, whose fat tastes the best? The lamb's!

SERVES 8

Cuttlefish (page 204)

Lime juice

Fennel–Lamb Fat Sauce (page 204)

2 bulbs baby fennel, thinly sliced

Fennel Bitters (page 204)

Olive oil

Kosher salt

About 24 pieces Black Garlic Feuilletine (page 205)

Maldon salt

1. Portion the cuttlefish into planks about ⅜ x ¾ inch. With a small, sharp knife, make 3 or 4 additional cuts that run parallel to the length of the plank, stopping just short of the end. The plank should remain intact. These incisions will allow you to fan the individual pieces as you plate them.

2. For each serving, place 3 pieces of the cuttlefish in a bowl, positioned at 12 o'clock, 4 o'clock, and 8 o'clock. Season each piece of cuttlefish with 2 drops of lime juice.

3. Sauce each plate with 1 dot of fennel–lamb fat sauce next to each piece of cuttlefish.

4. Dress the baby fennel with a drop each of the fennel bitters and olive oil and a pinch of kosher salt. Place a few pieces of baby fennel on each dot of fennel sauce.

5. Break the black garlic feuilletine into thumb-size pieces and place 1 piece over each pile of baby fennel. Season the cuttlefish with Maldon salt.

CUTTLEFISH

1 cuttlefish tail, about 900 grams
500 grams water
30 grams kosher salt

1. With a dry towel, clean the membrane off the cuttlefish. Place in a bowl. In a small bowl, whisk together the water and salt. Pour over the cuttlefish and brine for 10 minutes.
2. Rinse the fish and vacuum-seal in a cryovac bag. Cook sous vide in a 131°F water bath for 15 minutes. Cool in an ice bath. Refrigerate until ready to use.

RENDERED LAMB FAT

225 grams lamb fat (fat taken from the loin works well), diced
60 grams water

In a pot, combine the lamb fat and water. Bring the water nearly to a boil over medium heat, then reduce the heat to maintain a gentle simmer and cook until the fat has rendered and all of the water has evaporated, about 10 minutes. Pass through a tamis and chill over an ice bath. Discard any liquid that remains after rendering.

FENNEL–LAMB FAT SAUCE

20 grams star anise
200 grams fresh fennel, sliced
60 grams chicken stock
3 grams kosher salt, plus more as needed
100 grams Rendered Lamb Fat (recipe follows), rewarmed
0.55 gram (0.2%) xanthan gum

1. In a dry skillet, toast the star anise over medium heat until fragrant, about 1 minute.
2. Vacuum-seal the sliced fennel and star anise in a cryovac bag. Cook sous vide in a 194°F water bath for 40 minutes. Check for doneness—the fennel should be soft, without any resistance. Drain. Discard the star anise.
3. In a medium saucepan, heat the chicken stock over high heat to 140° to 170°F. Transfer the hot chicken stock to a blender. Add the fennel and salt and process until smooth. With the motor running, slowly drizzle in the warm lamb fat. Blend until emulsified. Taste and adjust the seasoning as needed.
4. Add the xanthan gum and blend on high speed for 10 seconds. Pass through a tamis and chill over an ice bath. Place in a squeeze bottle and hold in the refrigerator until ready to use.

FENNEL BITTERS

95 grams fresh fennel, sliced
Sugar
4 grams coriander seeds
4 grams star anise
4 grams fennel seeds
100 grams grain alcohol or neutral grain spirit (i.e., Everclear)
105 grams cold water

1. Sprinkle the fresh fennel generously with sugar and use a blowtorch to caramelize the sugar. Set aside in a large container.
2. In a dry pan over medium heat, toast the coriander seeds, star anise, and fennel seeds until fragrant, about 1 minute. Dump into the container with the brûléed fennel and mix to combine. Add the grain alcohol and water to the container and cover. Store in a dry, dark place for 10 days. Strain and hold at room temperature until ready to use.

BLACK GARLIC FEUILLETINE

270 grams whole milk

180 grams black garlic

182 grams all-purpose flour

8 grams baking soda

108 grams butter

22 grams sugar

1 egg, beaten

90 grams molasses

Cooking spray

1. In a small saucepan, heat the milk to a simmer. Add the garlic, cover the pot, remove from the heat, and let stand for 10 minutes. In a blender, process until smooth.

2. Sift together the flour and baking soda. Set aside.

3. In a stand mixer fitted with the paddle attachment, cream the butter and sugar until pale and fluffy, about 5 minutes. With the motor running, slowly add the beaten egg and mix to emulsify. Mix in the molasses, then slowly pour in the black garlic–milk mixture. Mix until smooth. Slowly add the dry ingredients and continue mixing until you have a thick pancake batter.

4. Heat the oven to 275°F.

5. Coat a silicone baking mat with cooking spray, then wipe it clean. Place on a sheet pan. Spread a 1/16-inch-thick layer of batter onto the mat. Bake for 7 minutes, then rotate the pan 180 degrees and bake for another 2 minutes.

6. Let the black garlic feuilletine cool at room temperature until crispy. Store in an airtight container until ready to use.

SOLE, BLACK LICORICE PIL PIL, FRIED GREEN TOMATO, FENNEL

This dish is a sentimental favorite because it tells Sam Henderson's story.

It's built around sole, but sole that Sam completely reimagined. In her early days at the restaurant, she'd seen us use meat glue to bind proteins into a tube shape, and through trial and error, she discovered that we could take a flat fish like turbot or sole and give it a completely different shape. We'd cut the fish into long strips, toss those in meat glue, and roll them into a cylinder, using plastic wrap to give them shape. We'd warm them in a CVap oven and then drop them in the fryer, just for a second, to create a contrast between the lightly crisped outside and the warm, pearlescent flesh inside.

Sam is from Atlanta, so she naturally paired fried things with more fried things— and fried green tomatoes are built into her DNA. Of course, Sam knows how I feel about tomatoes, which is that they are terrible and need significant processing to be edible at all. So Sam created a somewhat better tomato for this dish. She chopped green tomatoes, mixed them with a slurry of seasonings, meat glue, and gelatin, and set them in a sheet pan. Then she used a ring mold to cut out disks of this new-and-improved tomato to bread and fry.

The sauce is pil pil, a Basque sauce Sam learned to make at Mugaritz, where she worked during the years between leaving here an accomplished (but still young) cook and returning to run the kitchen as chef de cuisine. To make pil pil, you cook down the fatty, gelatinous parts of cod and then mount oil into it. The white version of this dish is fairly classic; the black one has licorice in it. We dragged it across the plate in a move we called the "tire track."

SERVES 6

Neutral oil

6 Fried Green Tomatoes (page 212)

6 portions Sole (page 212)

Black Licorice Sauce (page 212)

Licorice Pil Pil (page 213)

50 grams Pickled Baby Fennel (page 213)

Fennel fronds

1. Heat a large pot of oil to 375°F. Deep-fry the green tomatoes until golden brown, about 1 minute.

2. Flash the sole under the salamander until warmed through.

3. Drag black licorice sauce across the diameter of each plate, making a tire-track pattern. It will take practice to know how you should hold the spoon. Start with the blob and turn the spoon ever so slightly to get this effect (otherwise you just get a streak). Spoon 2 dots on one side of the line and 1 dot on the other.

4. Spoon 3 dots of pil pil around the plate. Lay a deep-fried tomato on the lower left side of the plate, or slice off an edge and stand it upright.

5. For each plate, slice a portion of fish on the bias. Stand one piece upright and lay the other on its side. Place baby fennel over the fish and garnish with fennel fronds.

FRIED GREEN TOMATOES

Batter Bind came to us through our connections with a company called Ingredion (formerly known as National Starch). The ingredient does exactly what the name suggests: It binds batter to whatever needs to be fried.

32 grams basil seeds

75 grams lemon vinegar

160 grams water

2 grams kosher salt

15 grams (5%) silver sheet gelatin, bloomed in ice water

6 grams (2%) Activa TI

250 grams coarsely chopped green tomatoes, seeded and drained

6 grams Ultra-Sperse 3

30 grams Batter Bind

1 egg, beaten

120 grams panko breadcrumbs, coarsely ground

1. In a small bowl, combine the basil seeds, vinegar, 100 grams of the water, and 0.5 gram of the salt. Let sit until the basil seeds are hydrated, about 5 minutes.
2. In a small bowl, warm 30 grams of the water, then dissolve the gelatin. In a separate bowl, hydrate the Activa in the remaining 30 grams of water.
3. In a large bowl, combine 45 grams of the hydrated basil seeds, the gelatin, Activa, green tomatoes, and Ultra-Sperse. Mix thoroughly with a rubber spatula.
4. Using a rolling pin, roll the mixture between sheets of plastic wrap to about ¼ inch thick. Refrigerate overnight.
5. Punch out disks of the tomato mixture with a 1½-inch ring cutter. Set aside.
6. Place the Batter Bind, egg, and panko in three separate bowls. Place a tomato disk in the Batter Bind, then in the egg, then in the panko, shaking off any excess. Place the disk back into the egg, then in the panko. Set aside. Repeat for all the disks. Refrigerate until ready to use.

SOLE

1 small lemon sole (about 900 grams), filleted

30 grams kosher salt

500 grams cold water

100 grams warm water (about 90°F)

25 grams Activa GS

10 grams Licorice Oil (page 212)

1. Cut the fish lengthwise into strips about ½ inch wide. Place in a bowl.
2. Mix together the salt and cold water and pour on top of the fish. Let sit for 5 minutes. Rinse and pat dry.
3. In a blender, process the warm water and Activa. Pour the mixture into a one-third hotel pan and place the open pan in a cryovac machine. Compress.
4. Coat the fish with the Activa slurry. Roll in plastic wrap into a long cylinder around 1 inch in diameter, like a torchon. Refrigerate for at least 2 hours to set.
5. Remove the fish from the plastic wrap, cut into 1½-inch plugs, and place each in a resealable plastic bag with 1½ teaspoons of licorice oil. (A cryovac bag will crush the shape of the fish.) Poach the fish in a 140°F water bath for 8 minutes. The fish should be cooked through but still tender; it should reveal an opalescent sheen when sliced.

BLACK LICORICE SAUCE

25 grams hard black licorice candy

60 grams soft black licorice candy

150 grams water

40 grams distilled white vinegar

50 grams strained aromatics from Licorice Oil (recipe follows)

38 grams cuttlefish ink

0.75 gram (0.2%) xanthan gum

150 grams Licorice Oil (recipe follows)

1. In a double boiler, combine both candies and 25 grams of the water. Cook until the licorice melts and a paste forms, about 5 minutes.
2. In a blender, process the black licorice paste, the remaining 125 grams of water, vinegar, aromatics, and cuttlefish ink until incorporated. Add the xanthan, then pour into a bowl.
3. Slowly whisk in the licorice oil until emulsified. Pass through a tamis. Refrigerate until ready to use.

LICORICE OIL

12 grams star anise

25 grams anise seeds

25 grams fennel seeds

12 grams licorice root

340 grams grapeseed oil

1. In a dry pan, toast the star anise, anise seeds, and fennel seeds until fragrant, about 1 minute.
2. In a blender, process the spices, licorice root, and oil on high for 2 minutes. Infuse at low heat for 12 hours: Place the oil in a pan in the oven with only the pilot light lit overnight. Strain, reserving the aromatics to make the Black Licorice Sauce (above). Refrigerate until ready to use.

LICORICE PIL PIL

65 grams Cod Skin Stock (recipe follows), chilled and gelatinous

1 gram kosher salt

20 grams lemon juice

3 grams lemon vinegar

88 grams Licorice Oil (below left)

In a bowl, whisk together the cod skin stock, salt, lemon juice, and vinegar. While whisking vigorously, slowly rain in the licorice oil and continue whisking until emulsified. Refrigerate until ready to use.

COD SKIN STOCK

910 grams cod skins, rinsed

Place the cod skins in a stockpot and add water to an inch below the level of the skins. Bring the water to a simmer and cook for 45 minutes, skimming the surface as necessary. Strain the stock and chill.

PICKLED BABY FENNEL

1 bulb baby fennel, thinly shaved

50 grams lemon vinegar

50 grams olive oil

Vacuum-seal the ingredients in a cryovac bag. Refrigerate until ready to use.

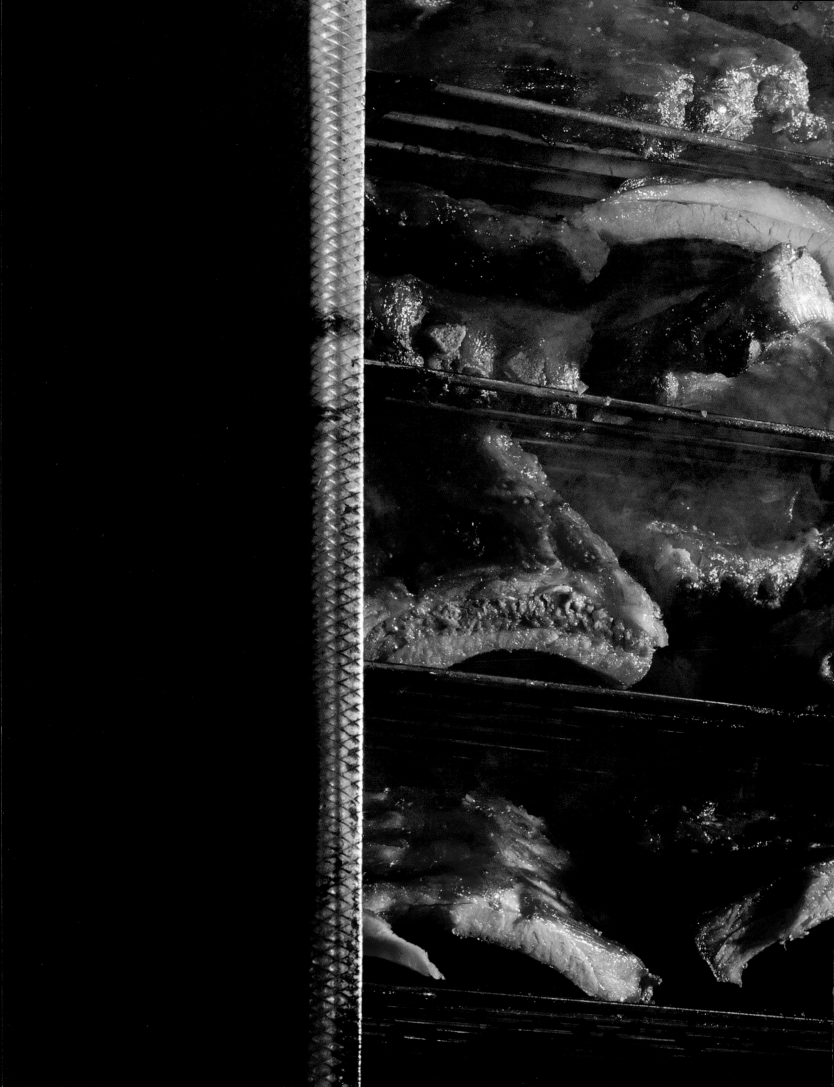

MEAT

CHICKEN, CARROT CONFIT, EGG YOLK, MOLE PAPER

This was an early meat glue experiment, and we called it the chicken ball. Our first sous-chef, Mike Sheerin, deboned and wrapped the chicken around itself, using meat glue to hold the whole thing together. We cooked it in three stages: first in a water bath to gently cook it through, then in a pan to develop the flavor, and finally in the deep fryer to crisp the skin. Rather than send it out as a whole ball, we cut a small section off so people could see inside.

We wanted the egg yolks on the plate to be the consistency of fudge, but back then, our methods were a little crude: We cooked the eggs whole, scraped off the white, then rolled out the yolks between plastic with a rolling pin. The finished dish was a play on textures: soft confit carrots, fudgy yolks, hot crisp chicken, and crunchy paper.

SERVES 6

Olive oil

20 pieces Carrot Confit (page 218)

Lemon juice

6 Egg Sheets (page 218)

Kosher salt

Freshly ground black pepper

6 Chicken Balls (page 218)

Mole Paper (page 219)

Red mustard sprouts

Chicken Jus (page 219)

1. Heat a large pot of oil to 350°F and heat the oven to 350°F.

2. In a small saucepan, warm the carrots with a splash of water and lemon juice over medium-low heat.

3. Place an egg sheet on each plate and season with salt, pepper, and olive oil. Place 5 pieces of the carrot confit on top of the egg sheet.

4. Deep-fry the chicken balls until the outside is crispy, 4 to 5 minutes. Move the chicken to a sheet pan and place in the oven until cooked through, about 10 minutes.

5. Cut off a small section of a chicken ball and place it to the side of the plate. Top the carrots with shards of mole paper and red mustard sprouts. Drizzle a little chicken jus on top of the bird and sprinkle with salt.

CARROT CONFIT

400 grams chicken fat

3 sprigs thyme

½ head garlic

1 fresh bay leaf

5 baby carrots, rainbow or otherwise, peeled,
    scrubbed, and cut into oblique shapes

1. In a saucepot, combine the chicken fat, thyme, garlic, and bay leaf and bring to about 170°F over low heat. Cook for 30 minutes.
2. Holding the temperature, add the carrots and cook until tender but not soft; a knife or cake tester should go through cleanly. This may take up to 30 minutes, depending on the carrots.

EGG SHEETS

4 eggs

1. Cook the eggs in a water bath at 147°F for 90 minutes. Shock in an ice bath and let cool.
2. Peel the eggs; discard the egg whites and any membrane surrounding the yolks. Pass the yolks through a tamis.
3. Place the yolk mixture between two pieces of plastic wrap or acetate and pound to the thickness of a slice of American cheese, about ⅛ inch.
4. Freeze the sheet of yolk, then cut it into four 1½ x 2½-inch rectangles. Return to the freezer until ready to serve.

CHICKEN BALLS

To make these chicken balls, we put the thinner part of the breast (the part most likely to dry out) on the inside so it stayed insulated and juicy through the cooking process.

3 whole chickens (about 1.2 kilograms each)

Kosher salt

Freshly ground black pepper

15 grams Activa RM

1. Bone each chicken, removing the breast, drumstick, and thigh in one piece. Remove the leg and thigh bones. Keep the meat in 4 separate half-bird piles.
2. Season the chicken with salt and pepper and sprinkle lightly with the Activa. To evenly distribute the meat glue, use a small sieve.
3. Working with a half chicken at a time, wrap the dark meat around the breast, shaping the meat into a ball as you go and making sure the skin is on the outside.
4. Wrap each meat ball tightly in plastic wrap. Twist and tie the plastic on either end and impale the ball several times with a cake tester to remove any air inside. Poach in a water bath at 147°F until the internal temperature reaches 143°F, 60 to 90 minutes. (To take the temperature, we used a fine digital probe, first putting a piece of tape over the spot where we were going to insert it—the same way you can put a Band-Aid on a balloon and pierce it without popping it.)
5. Let rest for 10 to 15 minutes, then place in an ice bath. Let cool. Refrigerate until ready to use, then remove the plastic.

MOLE PAPER

230 grams mole paste
300 grams water
100 grams simple syrup
1 egg white
Kosher salt
Cooking spray

In a blender, process the mole paste, water, simple syrup, egg white, and salt to taste until smooth. Spread on a silicone baking mat coated with cooking spray. Dry overnight in a dehydrator or in a convection oven set to 160°F.

CHICKEN JUS

1 kilogram chicken bones (wings and backs work well, as does the whole carcass)
1 head garlic, broken into cloves
2 medium Spanish onions, slivered
6 sprigs thyme
1 bay leaf
Water

1. Heat the oven to 425°F.
2. Lay the chicken bones on a roasting pan or sheet pan and roast until the bones are golden brown, about 45 minutes. Transfer the bones to a stockpot.
3. Deglaze the roasting pan with water, making sure to scrape the fond from the bottom. Add this liquid to the stockpot.
4. Add the garlic, onions, thyme, and bay leaf and sweat for a few minutes over medium heat. Fill the pot with water to just under the level of the bones. Simmer for 45 minutes and strain into a clean pot.
5. Bring the liquid to a rolling boil and reduce to about one-tenth of its original volume, skimming occasionally. Strain through a chinois. Let cool, then refrigerate until ready to use.

THE GENESIS OF PAPERS

Papers came about because we wanted to add something crispy to the plate other than traditional flour-based French tuiles. Chefs (and pastry chefs in particular) have always loved tuiles, but you can't get a big punch of flavor, because the excess of flour in the batter mutes whatever fruits or vegetables you add.

We wanted to make papers with intense flavor, so we started experimenting with egg whites and "low DE" sugars like maltodextrin and trehalose, to make tuiles that were less waferlike and more glassine. (DE means "dextrose equivalency," which is a bit of a strange measurement. We all know what sucrose, or table sugar, tastes like, but for reasons no one can explain, the scientific community's official scale of sugar sweetness is based on dextrose. It is, for the record, less sweet than sucrose.)

The reason we needed low-DE sugars instead of classic sucrose is that sucrose is hygroscopic: It's very effective at grabbing moisture out of the air, and while that's useful for some applications, ingredients made with sucrose tend to get soggy. These lower DE sugars are generally more resistant to humidity, which comes in handy when you want something to stay crisp.

My all-time favorite paper was one we made from hibiscus. We brewed a hibiscus tea, thickened it, then added maltodextrin, spread it out, and dried it out overnight. It looked like stained glass. We served it over a just-warm langoustine with triangles of endive and a purée of popcorn.

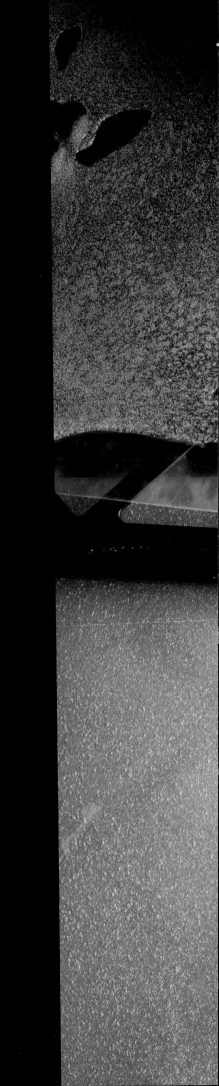

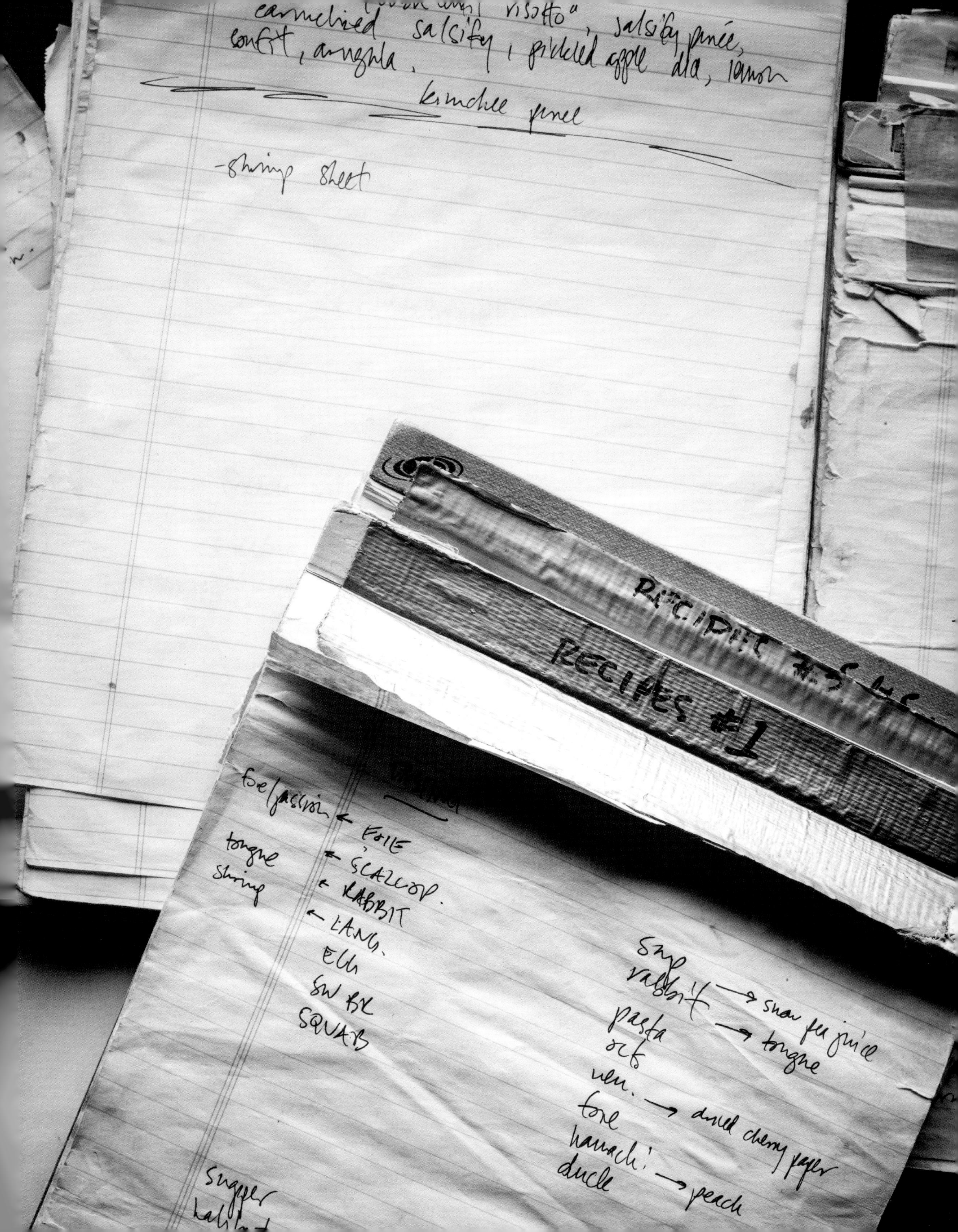

carmelized salsify + pickled apple dia, lemon
confit, arugula.

"___ ___ risotto", salsify puree,

kimchee puree

-shrimp sheet

RECIPES #5 ___

RECIPES #1

foie passion → FOIE
tongue → SCALLOP.
shrimp → RABBIT
→ LANG.
EEL
SW BX
SQUAB

shp
rabbit → snow pea juice
pasta → tongue
oct
ven.
foie → dried cherry paper
hamachi → peach
duck

sugar
rabbit

MORE ABOUT MEAT GLUE

Heston Blumenthal, chef/owner of the Fat Duck restaurant in England, introduced me to meat glue around 2003. The official name is transglutaminase, but Heston's crew called it meat glue, because that's really what it is: glue for meat. It's an enzyme that forms a covalent bond between certain proteins, and because it's safe (your body naturally makes the stuff) and has no discernible flavor, it became an incredibly useful tool in our kitchen.

When we reformed the flesh of a fish from an uneven natural shape into a cylinder or a block, we were able to cook the fish more evenly—and also guarantee that diners would never get a tough piece or cut through the meat in the wrong way.

At Jean-Georges, we used to make a rabbit sausage—diced rabbit meat, liver, and kidneys mixed with chicken and parsley and bound with egg. We wrapped that mixture in plastic, poached it, unmolded it, and sliced it. Most of the time the sausage held together, but sometimes it would fray or fall apart. When I first heard about meat glue, this was the dish that came to mind. I wanted to solve that problem and get perfect, sliceable, casingless sausages every time. So an updated version of Jean-Georges's rabbit sausage was our first meat glue dish.

While phase 1 of our meat glue work was about bonding piece A to piece B, later we started gluing ground protein to itself to give it a new shape, which is how we ended up with shrimp noodles. We also figured out how to make noodles out of puréed vegetables and grains. The amino acids required for meat glue to function were missing in these ingredients, but we realized we could add gelatin to solve that problem. This discovery led to pastas made almost entirely from puréed vegetables, quinoa glued together into deep-fried chips, and so on.

Our deployment of meat glue occasionally led to accusations of "playing God" in the kitchen, but we weren't making fantastical medieval beasts, and sparrows didn't fly out of our meat-glued chicken. Although honestly, I think that would have been awesome.

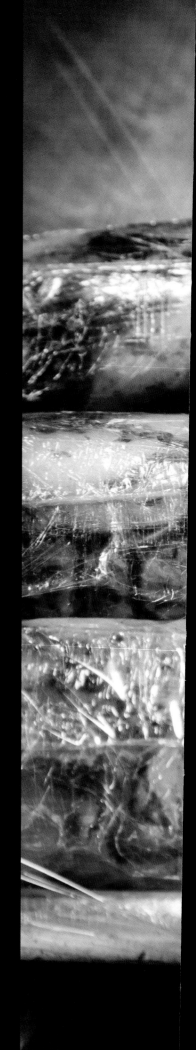

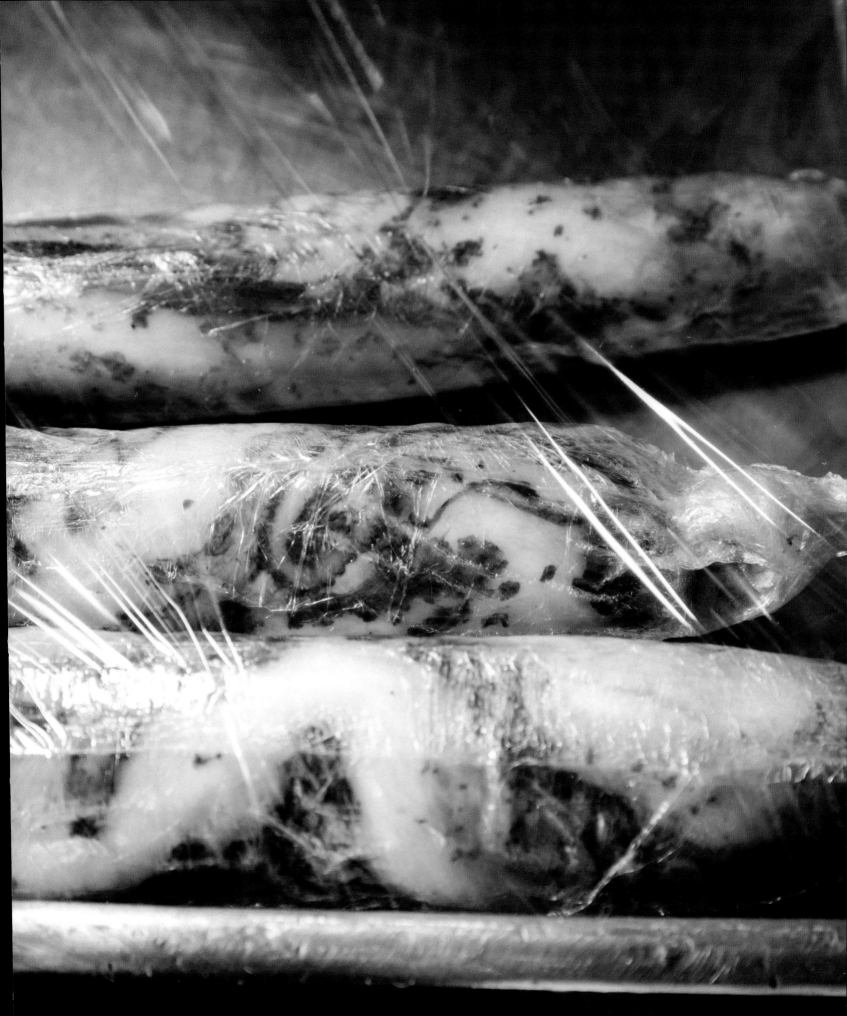

COLD FRIED CHICKEN, BUTTERMILK "RICOTTA," TABASCO, CAVIAR

Cold fried chicken is right up there with cold pizza on my list of favorite leftovers. I think it's as good as hot fried chicken. Jon Bignelli, a longtime part of the wd~50 kitchen, came up with the idea for a cold fried chicken course.

One frustrating thing about cold fried chicken is how the meat reacquaints itself with the bone and becomes difficult to separate, so we took the bone out. And we maximized the pleasure of the dish by making our fried chicken out of all thigh meat. We cooked large terrines of it sous vide, cut them into bars, and breaded and fried them just before service. Then we threw the chicken in the freezer to chill it quickly, so diners would get cold fried chicken that was still moist (because even the best fried chicken in the world dries out a little in the fridge overnight).

When we were staring at the almost-finished plate—chicken, Tabasco sauce, ricotta—I realized that caviar could make it a fun high-brow, low-brow dish.

SERVES 6

6 batons Cold Fried Chicken (page 228)
70 grams Tabasco Fluid Gel (page 229)
225 grams Buttermilk "Ricotta"
    (page 228)

12 pieces Crispy Chicken Skin (page 229)
75 grams hackleback caviar
12 chervil sprigs

1. For each serving, cut a piece of fried, chilled chicken in half and place the halves end-to-end (as though they're hinged) on a plate. Pipe 3 dots of Tabasco fluid gel around the chicken.

2. In a saucepan, stir the "ricotta" over medium heat to warm through. Place 3 spoonfuls around the chicken. Place a quenelle of caviar, about the size of a demitasse, over 1 pile of ricotta. Finish with 2 pieces of chicken skin and sprigs of chervil.

COLD FRIED CHICKEN

570 grams boneless, skinless chicken thighs

425 grams Standard Brine (see page 30)

25 grams Activa GS

100 grams warm water

BREADING

450 grams all-purpose flour

160 grams crushed cornflakes

150 grams cornstarch

15 grams baking powder

7 grams kosher salt

6 grams baking soda

13 grams sugar

150 grams Batter Bind

5 eggs, beaten

Neutral oil, for deep-frying

1. Combine the chicken and brine in a large container. Brine the chicken for 12 hours, making sure all of the pieces are submerged. Rinse and pat dry.

2. In a blender, process the Activa and water until dissolved. Place the Activa slurry in a vacuum chamber and compress around 5 times to remove air.

3. Coat the chicken thighs in the slurry. Layer the chicken into a terrine mold or a 4-inch-deep one-third pan (12.8 x 7 inches) and weight down to create a block. Let sit in the refrigerator for 2 to 3 hours.

4. Remove the set chicken block from the terrine mold and vacuum-seal in a cryovac bag. Cook sous vide in a 156°F water bath for 6 hours. Let cool.

5. Cut the chicken across the width of the block into 5 batonlike shapes. Trim the edges so you have those "hospital corners." Refrigerate until ready to use.

6. Make the breading: Combine all the ingredients in a large bowl.

7. Set out the Batter Bind, breading, and eggs in 3 separate bowls. Coat the chicken with the Batter Bind,

then dip into the egg wash, then into the breading. Dip once more in the egg wash and the breading.

8. Heat a large pot of oil to 375°F. Deep-fry the chicken pieces until golden brown, about 3 minutes. Let cool. Refrigerate until ready to use.

TABASCO FLUID GEL

This mixture is very shiny, with the texture of a classic Chinese takeout sauce.

35 grams Tabasco sauce

20 grams honey

195 grams water

0.75 grams (0.3%) xanthan gum

12 grams Ultra-Sperse 3

In a blender, process the Tabasco, honey, and water until smooth. Shear in the xanthan gum. Pour the mixture into a bowl and whisk in the Ultra-Sperse. Set aside until ready to use.

BUTTERMILK "RICOTTA"

This part of the dish could be challenging for the cooks: Sometimes it would come out looking more like cottage cheese than ricotta. Often, our cooks were from other countries, and they had no reference point for the correct size and texture of ricotta curds. So I'd use that as a chance to send them to Di Palo's, the greatest Italian cheese store in Manhattan, to taste the real thing. The fun trick about this particular technique is that when you heat the ricotta, it holds its structure.

300 grams buttermilk

100 grams sour cream

0.8 gram sodium hexametaphosphate

8 grams low-acyl gellan gum

0.2 gram calcium lactate

4 grams kosher salt

1. In a blender, process the buttermilk and sour cream until smooth. Shear in the sodium hexametaphosphate, then the gellan.
2. Pour the mixture into a saucepan and heat to 180°F over high heat. While whisking, add the calcium lactate and salt. Let cool.
3. Take one-third of the gel and blend until smooth. Chop the remaining gel until it resembles very small cheese curds. Combine the smooth gel and the chopped gel. Refrigerate until ready to use.

CRISPY CHICKEN SKIN

150 grams chicken skin

25 grams Activa GS

100 grams warm water

1. Carefully dry the chicken skins; if they are wet, the Activa will not adhere. (If you have the time, lay them on a dry towel atop a sheet pan in the refrigerator overnight.)
2. In a blender, shear the Activa into the water until dissolved. Place the slurry in a vacuum chamber and compress several times to remove air. Coat the chicken skins with the slurry, using a pastry brush to apply it.
3. Using plastic wrap, make a small torchon/cylinder of the skin, about 1½ inches in diameter. Twist the ends tightly and tie off. Impale several times with a cake tester to remove air. Let rest for 3 hours.
4. Place the torchon in an unsealed vacuum bag (vacuum-sealing would disfigure the shape), submerge in a 194°F water bath, and poach for 3 hours. Let cool, then freeze.
5. Heat the oven to 300°F.

6. Slice the chicken skin torchon on a deli slicer on setting #2. Place the slices between 2 silicone baking mats over an inverted half-sheet pan and bake until crispy, 30 minutes to 1 hour.

FRIED QUAIL, BANANA TARTAR, NASTURTIUM

The quail ball is the child of the chicken ball: boned-out quail shaped into an orb (with the help of meat glue), then poached, breaded, and fried.

We paired the quail with tartar sauce. Although most people think of tartar sauce as a seafood condiment, the British have historically served it alongside pigeon and similar fowl. Worcestershire sauce and anchovy are umami bombs that pair well with little birds.

Because cooking the quail ball didn't involve a sauté or roasting pan, we weren't left with any caramelized bits to make a sauce. Instead, we cooked the legs and made a jus for the plate, to add some of those roasted bird notes to the dish.

The final touch was nasturtium. I love the peppery quality of nasturtium—it has a bite that doesn't linger.

SERVES 6

1 banana

Banana Tartar Sauce (page 232)

Fried Quail (page 232)

Chicken Jus (page 219), warmed

Nasturtium leaves

1. Slice the banana into ¼-inch-thick coins, then halve the coins. Place 3 banana coin halves upright on each plate with about 1½ inches of space between them. Brûlé the bananas with a blowtorch and spoon some banana tartar sauce between them.

2. Cut each quail ball into 1 half and 2 quarters. Place the quail around the banana tartar sauce, sauce with chicken jus, and garnish with nasturtium leaves.

BANANA TARTAR SAUCE

Around the time we were putting the quail ball to-gether, Jon Bignelli and I had been experimenting with charred bananas, and Jon asked me if we should consider adding some to this dish, along with banana tartar sauce. I thought it was genius. Tartar sauce in-cludes a bunch of ingredients (like anchovies) that can be good foils to sweetness. We kept playing with tartar sauce over the years—we made an English pea ver-sion and, later, a ramp tartar sauce with fish and chips at Alder—but this one was always my favorite.

2 egg yolks

30 grams whole-grain mustard

300 grams grapeseed oil

30 grams capers

30 grams cornichons, minced

4 white anchovies, minced

12 grams chopped Italian parsley

12 grams chopped tarragon

5 bananas, chopped

Lemon juice

1. In a small food processor, blend the egg yolks and mustard until combined. With the motor running, slowly drizzle in the oil until emulsified.
2. Pour the mixture into a bowl and fold in the capers, cornichons, anchovies, parsley, tarragon, and ba-nanas. Season with lemon juice. Refrigerate until ready to use—it should be made the day of serving.

FRIED QUAIL

3 quail

2 to 5 grams Activa RM

125 grams all-purpose flour

2 eggs, beaten

100 grams panko breadcrumbs

Neutral oil, for deep-frying

1. Butcher each quail into two equal halves, cutting around the breast plate and leaving the skin on. Using a small knife, cut around the thigh bone and remove the bones from each of the legs, as well as any cartilage and sinew. Sprinkle the flesh side of each piece of quail lightly with the Activa. (Use a small sieve to evenly distribute the meat glue.)
2. Wrap the dark meat around the breast, shaping the meat into a ball as you go and making sure the skin is on the outside. Wrap the meat ball tightly in plas-tic wrap. Twist and tie the plastic on the bottom of the quail ball (where the ends come together) and puncture several times with a cake tester to release any air inside.
3. Poach in a 133°F water bath until the internal tem-perature reaches 133°F, about 45 minutes. (To take the temperature, we used a fine digital probe, first putting a piece of tape over the spot where we were going to insert it—the same way you can put a Band-Aid on a balloon and pierce it without pop-ping it.) Let rest for 10 to 15 minutes, then cool in an ice bath. Refrigerate until ready to use.
4. Remove the plastic from the quail balls. Set out the flour, eggs, and panko in 3 separate bowls. Coat the quail balls in the flour, then in the egg, then in the panko.
5. Heat a large pot of oil to 375°F. Deep-fry the quail balls until golden brown, 1 to 2 minutes. Rest 3 min-utes and then serve.

DUCK PROSCIUTTO, NORI PEANUT BUTTER, PICKLED CARROT, BRIOCHE

The genesis of the duck prosciutto was fairly juvenile: J.J. and I were talking about making cured meats and we thought, *How awesome would it be if we hung meats in Dewey's wine cellar? How angry do you think that would make him?* Dewey is Wylie's dad, and the cellar was his man cave. It was also the private dining room, and the décor included a huge metal GROCERY sign from the bodega that was at 50 Clinton Street before the restaurant. There were empty wine cubbies behind the sign, so we hung our meat in there. One night, Dewey took down the sign to do inventory and saw a bunch of ducks hanging from the ceiling. He wasn't thrilled, but he liked the prosciutto so much, he let us keep doing it.

Before we hung the duck in the cellar, we would cure it for two days. We used a lot of pink peppercorn and sansho in the cure, which gave the meat an interesting brightness that prosciutto doesn't usually have. We'd hang it for about two weeks, throw it in the fridge for a couple of days, and finally torch the skin.

Pairing the nori peanut butter with the prosciutto was kind of like putting Sriracha on a cream puff: It seemed like a really bad idea, but it worked. And the pickled carrot added crunch and acid. This dish wasn't on the menu, but we sent it out to friends from the kitchen.

—Sam Henderson

SERVES 8 TO 10 (EACH SERVING A SINGLE BITE)

Duck Prosciutto (page 236)
Pickled Carrot (page 237)
8 to 10 pieces Brioche (page 236), roughly
  1½ x ½ x ¼ inches

4 to 5 tablespoons Nori Peanut Butter
  (page 237)
Micro shiso

1. On a deli slicer, thinly slice 3 lengthwise pieces of duck prosciutto per plate. Cut 24 to 30 small, pennant-shaped triangles out of the pickled carrot. Set aside.

2. Toast the brioche slices and spread each with 1½ teaspoons of nori peanut butter.

3. Stand the duck pieces skin side up on a plate and twist in a tight, serpentine manner. Lay 3 or 4 pieces of pickled carrot on top and garnish with micro shiso. Move this on top of the brioche.

DUCK PROSCIUTTO

1 duck breast (we used Crescent Pekin; other ducks,
    such as Rohan or Moulard, may be used, but you
    will have to adjust the curing time to size)
Instacure #2
40 grams kosher salt
40 grams sugar
6 grams Bay Leaf Powder (recipe follows)
5 grams pink peppercorns, ground
0.5 gram dried sansho pepper

1. Weigh the duck breast and calculate 0.3% of
   the weight. Measure out that weight in Instacure
   #2 and set aside.
2. In a small bowl, combine the salt, sugar, bay leaf
   powder, pink peppercorns, and sansho pepper.
   Rub the duck breast with the Instacure #2, then
   the curing mix. Vacuum-seal the breast in a cryovac bag and place in the refrigerator to cure for
   2 days, turning once after the first day.
3. Rinse the duck breast well and let dry in the refrigerator for 2 more days.
4. Wrap the breast in cheesecloth and weigh. Hang
   in a temperate, relatively dry place—65° to 68°F
   works well. Once the ducks have lost one-third of
   their weight, pull them down; this should take 7 to
   10 days.
5. Cool the duck in the refrigerator for a day. Brûlé
   the skin with a blowtorch, then vacuum-seal the
   duck breast back in a cryovac bag. Refrigerate
   until ready to use.

BAY LEAF POWDER

30 grams bay leaves

Pour liquid nitrogen over the bay leaves to cryo-freeze
them. Blend to a powder and pass through a tamis.

BRIOCHE

15 grams active dried yeast
90 grams sugar
105 grams whole milk
7 eggs
750 grams all-purpose flour
22 grams kosher salt
300 grams cold unsalted butter, cut into 1-inch
    cubes
Cooking spray

1. In a bowl, combine the yeast and 1.5 grams of the
   sugar.
2. Warm the milk to about 70°F and pour it over the
   yeast and sugar. Whisk until bubbles form. Wrap
   the bowl in plastic and leave in a warm place for
   10 minutes.
3. Pour the yeast mixture into the bowl of a stand
   mixer fitted with the dough hook. Add the eggs
   and flour and mix on low speed for 1 minute.
4. Add the remaining sugar and the salt and mix on
   medium speed for 10 minutes.
5. Add the butter, one piece at a time, until fully incorporated.
6. Transfer the dough to a plastic container coated
   with cooking spray. Cover with plastic. Proof for
   8 hours, or overnight in the refrigerator.
7. Heat the oven to 350°F.
8. Knead the dough and shape it to fit inside of a Pull-
   man loaf pan. Proof with the lid on in a warm area
   until the dough rises to the top of the pan.
9. Bake for 45 minutes. Let cool.

NORI PEANUT BUTTER

180 grams unsalted roasted peanuts

5 grams nori, ground to a powder

22 grams brown sugar

18 grams grilled peanut oil

2 grams kosher salt

In a food processor, blend the ingredients until the texture resembles a natural, but spreadable, peanut butter.

PICKLED CARROT

100 grams water

25 grams lemon vinegar

2 grams kosher salt

1 medium carrot, peeled

1. In a medium bowl, combine the water, vinegar, and salt. Set aside.
2. Shave the carrot lengthwise into very thin strips. Bring a stockpot of salted water to a boil. Blanch the carrot shavings until al dente, 3 to 5 minutes. Shock in ice water. Let cool.
3. Vacuum-seal the carrot shavings and pickling liquid in a cryovac bag. Refrigerate until ready to use.

PORK COLLAR, POPPY SEEDS, RED BELL PEPPER, TAMARIND

SERVES 6

30 grams butter, plus more as needed

2 cloves garlic

3 sprigs thyme

2 small torchons Pork Neck (page 242)

6 disks Purple-Top Turnips (page 242)

Olive oil

Kosher salt

Red Bell Pepper Relish (page 243)

6 sheets Poppy Seed "Skin" (page 243)

25 grams Poppy Seed Crumble (page 244)

12 sprigs delfino cilantro

Pork Tamarind Sauce (page 244)

1. Heat the oven to 350°F.

2. In a black steel pan, melt the butter and add the garlic and thyme. Sear the pork torchons until browned, about 2 minutes per side. Baste a few times with the butter and place in the oven until warmed through, about 10 minutes. Set aside and let rest. Slice into ¾-inch-thick coins.

3. Heat a plancha or cast-iron skillet until ripping hot. Char the turnips until semi-blackened on one side, about 1 minute. Drizzle with olive oil and season with salt.

4. Place a turnip on each plate. Follow with a spoonful of relish. Gently warm the poppy seed skin on a small tray under a salamander with a bit of butter and place a slice on top of the relish. Place 3 slices of pork next to the skin. Garnish the rest of the plate with 1 teaspoon of poppy seed crumble and 2 sprigs of delfino. Sauce the pork with the pork tamarind sauce.

PORK NECK

25 grams kosher salt

20 grams sugar

3.75 grams Instacure #1

10 juniper berries, toasted

1 bay leaf

1 kilogram water

910 grams pork neck meat, trimmed of gland and sinew

25 grams Activa GS

1. In a saucepan, combine the salt, sugar, Instacure, juniper berries, bay leaf, and water. Bring to a boil to dissolve, then let the brine cool.
2. Cut the cleaned pork into strips roughly ½ inch thick. Place the pork in a large container and pour the brine over to submerge. Refrigerate for 24 hours. Rinse and pat dry.
3. Pull 100 grams of warm (90° to 100°F) water from the tap. Mix with the Activa in a blender. Place in an open container in a vacuum chamber and compress twice to remove air (you will have to hit stop before the cycle completes to prevent overflow).
4. In a bowl, combine the pork and enough Activa slurry to coat completely.
5. Lay plastic wrap down on a countertop, place half the meat on top, and roll into a torchon/cylinder, pinching the ends as you roll to tighten. Tie off the ends and puncture with a cake tester to release air. Repeat with the remaining meat and refrigerate overnight before cooking.

PURPLE-TOP TURNIPS

2 medium purple-top turnips

2 tablespoons Flavored Oil (recipe follows)

1. Leaving the skin on, slice the turnips into coins about ⅓ inch thick. Lay the turnips flat in a cryovac bag with the flavored oil and vacuum-seal. Cook sous vide in a 194°F water bath for 11 minutes.
2. Punch coins out of the turnips with a 1-inch ring mold. Set aside.

FLAVORED OIL

5 cloves garlic, smashed

1 medium carrot, thinly sliced

20 sprigs thyme

225 grams pork fat

240 grams olive oil

3 bay leaves

4 grams black peppercorns

In a small saucepan, combine all the ingredients and bring to a boil. Cover, remove from the heat, and let steep for 1 hour. Strain and refrigerate until ready to use.

RED BELL PEPPER RELISH

100 grams roasted red bell pepper, finely diced

15 grams Pressure-Cooked Poppy Seeds (page 244)

50 grams fresh red bell pepper, finely diced

15 grams Honey Garlic (page 26), minced

5 grams cilantro, thin stems included, chiffonade

5 grams kosher salt, or more to taste

Place the roasted bell pepper, poppy seeds, fresh bell pepper, honey garlic, cilantro, and salt in a mortar and crush with a pestle until everything is mixed but not ground into a paste. Season with the salt.

POPPY SEED "SKIN"

72 grams water

2 grams Activa TI

2 grams Activa RM

10 grams silver sheet gelatin, bloomed in ice water

12 grams poppy seed oil (or neutral oil, like canola)

150 grams Poppy Seed Butter (page 244)

1. Divide the water equally between two small pots. Bring one pot to 96°F and whisk in the Activa TI and Activa RM. Bring the other pot to 140°F and whisk in the gelatin until dissolved.

2. Whisk the two solutions together and pour into a blender. Blend on medium speed. With the motor running, drizzle in the oil, then add the poppy seed butter. Blend until the mixture becomes a thick purée.

3. At this point you must work quickly or the gelatin will begin to set. Stretch a piece of plastic wrap on a damp countertop and place half of the purée onto the middle. Cover the purée with another piece of plastic and smooth it over with your hands to remove the air. Using a rolling pin, gently roll the purée into thin sheets (almost paper-thin).

With a buddy, pull the sheet at its corners and stretch tight to prevent wrinkles from forming. Line a sheet pan with acetate, place the sheet of poppy seed skin on top of the acetate, then place another sheet of acetate on top. Repeat with the remaining purée to make a second sheet. Let cool overnight to set.

4. To portion, remove the plastic and cut the poppy seed skin into 2 x 3-inch rectangles. Refrigerate on sheets of parchment until ready to use.

POPPY SEED BUTTER

110 grams Pressure-Cooked Poppy Seeds (page 244)

355 grams water

75 grams pork fat

65 grams poppy seed oil

In a blender, process the cooked poppy seeds, water, pork fat, and poppy seed oil until smooth. Refrigerate until ready to use.

POPPY SEED CRUMBLE

Neutral oil, for deep-frying
200 grams Pressure-Cooked Poppy Seeds (recipe follows), patted dry
100 grams isomalt, ground to a fine powder

1. Heat a pot of oil to 375°F. Heat the oven to 350°F.
2. Deep-fry the poppy seeds until crunchy, about 2 minutes. Pat down on paper towels.
3. In a bowl, combine the fried poppy seeds and iso-malt. Spread the poppy–isomalt mixture between 2 silicone baking mats. Bake until the isomalt adheres to the seeds, about 45 minutes. Hold at room temperature until ready to use.

PRESSURE-COOKED POPPY SEEDS

170 grams white poppy seeds
710 grams water

Place the white poppy seeds and water in a pressure cooker and cook for 1 to 1½ hours. When they're done, the poppy seeds should yield to your teeth without too much resistance.

PORK TAMARIND SAUCE

225 grams tamarind paste
450 grams hot water
50 grams red miso
0.5 gram (0.2%) xanthan gum
300 grams Pork Jus (refer to Chicken Jus on page 219, but use pork stew meat or pork bones in place of the chicken), warmed

1. Steep the tamarind in the hot water for 1 hour, breaking the paste apart as it softens. Strain, being careful not to push the liquid through the chinois; you want it to drain naturally. Measure out 200 grams of the tamarind water. (If any remains, it makes a tasty drink with a little sugar added.)
2. In a blender, process the tamarind water and red miso. While blending, shear in the xanthan gum. Warm the pork jus until liquid. Place the tamarind mixture and pork jus in a bowl and whisk together gently.

LAMB LOIN, BLACK GARLIC ROMESCO, SOYBEAN, PICKLED GARLIC CHIVE

This dish was inspired by Spain's popular *calçotadas*: springtime beer hall events where long tables are outfitted with huge buckets of romesco, and everyone eats charred calçots (similar to scallions). The calçots are wrapped in newspaper and thrown onto a fire, so the whole thing burns and smolders. You then slide the charred bits off the calçots and there's a perfectly cooked onion underneath that you dip in the romesco.

I thought I could play off the ingredients in romesco for this dish, and instead of focusing on the red pepper I'd focus on garlic—or black garlic, in this case. Then we added the calçot of New York: the ramp. Ramps grow wild and get bigger as the season progresses. At first, they're like thin scallions; later they develop a bulb and a thicker stem and they're less magical. So I arranged a deal with one of my favorite farmers, Rick Bishop, who gave me dibs on the first three weeks of the ramp harvest. We'd clean them, pickle them whole, and put a couple on the plate with a smear of black garlic romesco and a dab of lamb jus. The flavors were good, but everything was kind of soft, so we added black edamame. We'd been drying them to use in soup, so we put them back in a pan with a little water and they became almost chewy—not fully dried but not fully rehydrated, either.

SERVES 6

18 to 24 ounces lamb loin, about 550 to
    650 grams, cut into 6 portions
Butter
3 or 4 sprigs thyme
1 clove garlic
15 grams water
Black Edamame (page 249)

Pickled Ramps (page 249)
Black Garlic Romesco (page 249)
Basil
Lamb Jus (refer to Chicken Jus on
    page 219, but use lamb stew meat or
    lamb bones in place of the chicken),
    warmed

1. Heat the oven to 350°F.

2. Place the lamb portions in a medium-hot black steel pan. Render the fat over medium heat, draining the pan constantly (save this fat!). Once the fat cap has rendered down to about ¼ inch, add a pat of butter, the thyme, and the garlic and baste the loins 3 or 4 times. Place the pan in the oven until a cake tester inserted into the flesh feels warm to the touch, 6 to 12 minutes. Remove the lamb from the oven and place on a resting rack.

3. In a sauté pan, warm a pat of butter and the water over medium heat. Add 3 to 4 tablespoons of black edamame and 3 to 4 tablespoons of pickled ramps. Cook, stirring, until warmed through.

4. For each serving, with a small offset spatula, swipe the center of a plate with romesco; the pattern should resemble a wave. Place a lamb portion perpendicular to the romesco. Cascade the warmed soybeans and ramps from the corner of the lamb. Garnish with basil and lamb jus.

BAAAAAAAA!

Lamb is my favorite meat, and I mean that in every way. I love prepping it, cooking it, eating it. There's something about cooking lamb that I find satisfying: learning how to sear it, baste it, put it in and take it out of the oven, press the cake tester against your lower lip to check the doneness. There's nothing particularly modern about this process—it's just good old-fashioned cooking.

I also love lamb because the fat is insanely delicious. At wd~50 we started leaving thicker and thicker caps of it on the meat. It was a risky move. If we didn't sear the fat enough, it was flabby and people would be turned off, but when we got it right it was crunchy like a crackling, and it amplified the flavor of the lamb.

BLACK EDAMAME

500 grams black edamame, hulled

In a food processor, pulse the edamame until they look like crushed nuts. Spread evenly on a dehydrator tray and dry at 145° to 150°F until brittle, 4 to 6 hours.

PICKLED RAMPS

This is an old recipe that I used at 71 Clinton Fresh Food. We poured the hot pickling liquid over buckets of ramps and just let them sit.

2 bunches ramps (garlic chives will work if it is not
    ramp season), cleaned
2 whole cloves
4 grams yellow mustard seeds
4 grams black peppercorns
5 grams coriander seeds
1 gram red chili flakes
455 grams water
225 grams rice vinegar
160 grams sugar
20 grams kosher salt
15 grams chopped fresh ginger

1. Place the ramps in a large bowl or plastic container.
2. In a dry skillet, toast the cloves, mustard seeds, peppercorns, coriander seeds, and chili flakes until fragrant, about 1 minute.
3. In a medium saucepan, combine the water, vinegar, sugar, salt, ginger, and toasted spices. Bring to a boil and remove from the heat. Let steep for 45 minutes. Strain the mixture into a clean saucepan and return to a boil. Pour the liquid over the ramps.
4. Let stand for at least 3 days. Remove the ramps from the liquid and chop into ¼-inch pieces.

BLACK GARLIC ROMESCO

170 grams black garlic
50 grams sliced almonds, toasted
10 grams chipotle peppers, hydrated and seeded
30 grams olive oil
0.26 gram (0.1%) xanthan gum
Kosher salt

In a food processor, combine the black garlic, almonds, and chipotles and pulse until you have a chunky paste. Drizzle in the oil and pulse to combine. Pour the mixture into a bowl and whisk in the xanthan gum. Season with salt to taste. Refrigerate until ready to use.

LAMB BELLY, BLACK CHICKPEA, CHERRIED CUCUMBER

SERVES 6

18 to 24 slices Lamb Belly (page 252)

Black Chickpea Hummus (page 252)

Cherry Cucumber Noodles (page 252)

Candied Chickpeas (page 253)

Micro lemongrass

1. Heat a black steel pan over high heat. Sear the lamb belly until crispy, about 2 minutes.

2. Warm the chickpea hummus in a small saucepan, stirring with a rubber spatula.

3. Warm the cherry cucumber noodles under a salamander.

4. Place 3 or 4 slices of lamb in the center of each plate. Spoon hummus on one side of the lamb and place a small pile of cucumber noodles on the other. Scatter the plate with candied chickpeas and top with micro lemongrass.

LAMB BELLY

200 grams kosher salt

200 grams brown sugar

25 grams Instacure #2

1 lamb belly, cleaned, ribs removed

1. In a small bowl, combine the salt, brown sugar, and Instacure. Coat the lamb belly thoroughly on both sides and refrigerate for 48 hours. Rinse thoroughly.
2. Vacuum-seal the lamb belly in a cryovac bag. Cook sous vide in a 156°F water bath until tender, about 12 hours. Transfer to an ice bath and weigh down so the belly lays flat; let cool.
3. Slice the belly on a deli slicer as you would thick-cut bacon. Refrigerate until ready to use.

BLACK CHICKPEA HUMMUS

200 grams black chickpeas

750 grams Parmesan Broth (recipe follows)

Kosher salt

1. Soak the chickpeas in water overnight. Drain (discard the soaking water).
2. Cook the chickpeas and Parmesan broth in a pressure cooker for 45 minutes. Drain the chickpeas, reserving the cooking liquid.
3. Set aside 100 grams of cooked chickpeas for the Candied Chickpeas (page 253). Purée the remaining chickpeas, adding the cooking liquid as needed to get the desired texture. (It should be the thickness of hummus.) Season with salt and place over an ice bath. Lay a piece of plastic over the top to prevent skinning up. Let cool, then refrigerate until ready to use.

PARMESAN BROTH

1 small onion

1 stalk celery

1 head garlic, halved

1 bunch thyme

250 grams Grana Padano cheese, cut into large chunks

250 grams Parmesan rind, cut into large chunks

1. Wrap the onion, celery, garlic, and thyme in cheesecloth. Place the bundle and cheese in a large stockpot and add water to cover by 2 inches. Bring to a boil, then reduce to a very low simmer. Cook, uncovered, for 2 hours.
2. Strain the broth, reserving the aromatics and cheese. Place the aromatics and cheese in a pot, cover with fresh water by 2 inches, and cook at a very low simmer, uncovered, for 3 hours. Combine the 2 batches of stock and let cool. Refrigerate until ready to use.

CHERRY CUCUMBER NOODLES

100 grams cucumbers, julienned

150 grams cherry purée

Vacuum-seal the cucumbers and purée in a cryovac bag. Remove from the cryovac bag and drain off any excess cherry purée. Refrigerate until ready to use.

CANDIED CHICKPEAS

100 grams cooked black chickpeas (from Black
  Chickpea Hummus, page 252)
Neutral oil, for deep-frying
30 grams Isomalt Caramel Powder (recipe follows)

1. Lay the cooked chickpeas on a sheet pan lined with paper towels and let dry at room temperature for at least 3 hours.
2. Heat a pot of oil to 375°F. Deep-fry the chickpeas until they have all puffed, but none have burned, about 3 minutes. Pat down on paper towels and hold in a warm, dry spot (such as a plate-warming drawer).
3. Heat the oven to 350°F. Line a sheet pan with a silicone baking mat.
4. In a large bowl, toss together the chickpeas and caramel powder. Sift off any excess powder and lay the chickpeas on the sheet pan. Bake until the sugar has melted, 4 to 5 minutes, tossing a few times so they don't stick together. Let cool, then store in an airtight container with a desiccant pack.

ISOMALT CARAMEL POWDER

50 grams glucose syrup
50 grams isomalt
50 grams sugar

1. In a saucepan, combine the glucose, isomalt, and sugar and bring to 313°F. Let cool. The mixture should become solid.
2. In a food processor, blend the mixture to a powder. Pass through a tamis and store in an airtight container with a desiccant pack.

WAGYU FLAT IRON, BEEF TENDON, WATERMELON, CARAMELIZED ONION

Meat purveyors are always trying to figure out new ways to cut up an animal, and that's how this dish came to be. I was buying a lot of hanger steak from Gachot & Gachot, a family business in New York's Meatpacking District, and Chris Gachot came to me with a cut he was calling a flat iron steak. He named it that because it was a wide, flat piece of meat with a heavy-duty piece of silver skin running through it.

We didn't want to make stew out of the steak, which would have been the easiest way to cook tough silver skin into submission. Instead, we butchered the flat iron, cutting out that piece of silver skin and gluing the steak back together into a little loaf. At the time, we were cooking many meats sous vide, but Mike Sheerin and I decided we wanted to cook the flat iron the old-fashioned way, by gently searing it. We had to be careful not to burn the spice mix on the outside of the steak, though, so we had to turn it constantly.

The flat iron steak became the go-to steak at wd~50. I'll never forget the day I was home watching TV and I saw an ad that said, "Come to TGI Fridays for flat iron steaks!" I thought, *Wow, things really do trickle down.* Flat iron steaks at TGI Fridays. Cool.

SERVES 20

(YES, THIS IS A LOT, BUT IT IS BEST TO START WITH ONE TRUE FLAT IRON.)

10 portions Wagyu (page 257)

Black Bean/Jerky Powder (page 257)

Kosher salt

Clarified butter

60 slices Watermelon Radish (page 258)

40 slices Steamed Watermelon
    (page 258)

Caramelized Onion Purée (page 258)

Beef Jus (refer to Chicken Jus on
    page 219, but use beef stew meat or
    beef bones in place of the chicken),
    warmed

20 Puffed Black-Bean Beef Tendons
    (page 259)

1. Heat the oven to 350°F.

2. Roll the portions of wagyu in the black bean/jerky powder and season with salt.

3. Heat a cast-iron pan over high heat until smoking. Add a slick of clarified butter and, working in batches, sear all sides of each portion of wagyu until evenly charred, just a couple of seconds. (Your pan will continue smoking while you do this.) Transfer the meat to a sheet pan, place in the oven, and cook, turning often, until medium-rare, 10 to 14 minutes. Probe the steak with a cake tester and pull out the steak when the tester is warm to the touch.

4. Warm the watermelon radish and steamed watermelon under a salamander.

5. For each serving, dust a plate with black bean/jerky powder. Pipe 3 dots of caramelized onion purée in the middle of the plate and lay 3 pieces of radish and 3 pieces of watermelon on top. Slice each steak portion into 2 pieces and lay 1 piece on each plate. Dress with beef jus. Garnish each plate with 1 puffed beef tendon.

WAGYU

1 wagyu flat iron steak, about 675 grams

100 grams water, warmed to between 90° and 100°F

25 grams Activa GS

1. Flat iron cuts have one large central piece of silver skin running through the middle of the steak. Remove this and any additional sinew and arteries; you will need to separate the top and bottom layers to completely remove the silver skin.
2. Place the water in a blender and stream in the Activa. Blend quickly, for about 15 seconds—you don't want to inject too much air into the mixture. Compress the Activa slurry in a vacuum chamber to remove any air.
3. Brush both sides of the meat with the Activa slurry and lay one on top of the other. Wrap tightly in plastic, then vacuum-seal in a cryovac bag. Weigh down and refrigerate for at least 3 hours. Slice into 85-gram portions (each portion will yield enough for two tasting-size dishes).

BLACK BEAN/ JERKY POWDER

1 part Jerky Powder (recipe follows)

1 part Fermented Black Bean Powder (page 258)

Combine the two powders.

JERKY POWDER

2 heads pioppini mushrooms

455 grams cherrywood chips

75 grams soy sauce

100 grams water

25 grams mirin

30 grams Worcestershire sauce

40 grams brown sugar

2 grams onion powder

2 grams garlic powder

0.5 gram freshly ground black pepper

1. Trim the mushrooms and remove any grit. Lay them in a single layer in a perforated hotel pan, place in the smoker, and smoke until the chips have expired, 15 to 20 minutes.
2. In a large saucepan, combine the soy sauce, water, mirin, Worcestershire sauce, brown sugar, onion powder, garlic powder, and pepper. Bring to a boil, whisking to dissolve. Let cool.
3. Vacuum-seal the smoked mushrooms and marinade in a cryovac bag and let infuse for 24 hours. Drain.
4. Spread the mushrooms onto a sheet pan. Dehydrate at 150° to 160°F until brittle; this is best done overnight in an oven with only the pilot light on. Pulverize in a blender.

FERMENTED BLACK BEAN POWDER

I find joy in the deep, funky flavors of mole, vadouvan, black garlic, and pretty much anything fermented. To make this powder, we rinsed fermented black beans, put them in the dehydrator until they were crunchy, and then pulverized them. Once we had a powder, we could use it as a flavoring agent the way you might use cinnamon or nutmeg. (Try folding it into butter and spreading it on toast—it's like Marmite but so much better.)

910 grams fermented black beans, rinsed well

1. Spread the fermented black beans over a sheet pan. Dry the beans in a low oven or dehydrator at 150° to 160°F until brittle, overnight.
2. Pulverize in a blender.

WATERMELON RADISH

2 medium watermelon radishes

100 grams water

25 grams lemon vinegar

10 grams lemon juice

2 grams kosher salt

5 grams sugar

1. Peel the radishes and shave them into paper-thin slices on a mandoline or deli slicer.
2. In a small saucepan, combine the water, vinegar, lemon juice, salt, and sugar. Heat the mixture over low heat, stirring, until the sugar dissolves. Let cool.
3. Vacuum-seal the radishes and liquid in a cryovac bag. Refrigerate until ready to use.

STEAMED WATERMELON

½ small watermelon, skin, rind, and seeds removed, cut into quarters

200 grams wood chips

1.6 liters water

100 grams tamari

Kosher salt

1. Place the watermelon in the freezer for about 20 minutes. Once the melon is sturdy, shave it on a deli slicer to about ⅛ inch thick. Arrange in shingles in a perforated hotel pan and set aside.
2. Lay the wood chips in a single layer on a half-sheet pan and toast under a salamander until smoldering. Transfer the smoldering chips to a full hotel pan, add the water and tamari, and bring to a simmer. Season the watermelon gently with salt and place over the simmering water. Steam, covered, for 1½ minutes. Let cool. Refrigerate until ready to use.

CARAMELIZED ONION PURÉE

2 medium Spanish onions, slivered

3 grams Black Bean/Jerky Powder (page 257)

Kosher salt

10 grams olive oil

Xanthan gum

1. Season the onions with the black bean/jerky powder and salt.
2. In a stainless steel pan, heat the oil over medium heat. Throw in the onions and cook, stirring, until tender and caramelized, about 15 minutes. Deglaze the pan with water as necessary.
3. Weigh the cooked onions and measure out 0.2% of

that weight in xanthan gum. Transfer the onions to a blender and process on high until smooth, then add the xanthan gum. Pass the mixture through a chinois, then cool over an ice bath. Place the mixture in a squeeze bottle and refrigerate until ready to use.

PUFFED BLACK-BEAN BEEF TENDONS

910 grams beef tendons

1 head garlic, halved

2 bay leaves

5 sprigs thyme

Fermented Black Bean Powder (page 258)

Cooking spray

Neutral oil, for deep-frying

1. Vacuum-seal the beef tendons, garlic, bay leaves, and thyme in a cryovac bag. Cook sous vide in a 194°F water bath for 20 hours. The tendon should be "hammered" (your finger should pierce the meat easily). Drain.
2. Weigh the tendons. Measure out 100 grams of fermented black bean powder for every 400 grams of cooked tendon.
3. Meanwhile, cut 10 strips of acetate that measure 2 x 10 inches. Coat with cooking spray and wipe with a paper towel.
4. In a blender, process the beef tendons and black bean powder until smooth. Pass through a tamis quickly, keeping the mixture hot.
5. Spread the tendon base in a very thin layer on top of the acetate strips. Let dry at room temperature until brittle—this will take 8 to 12 hours. Break into 2-inch squares.
6. Heat a pot of oil to 375°F. Deep-fry the tendon pieces until puffy, about 30 seconds. Pat down on paper towels. Set aside until ready to use.

CORNED BEEF CHEEK, TENDON, BANANA-HORSERADISH, MYOGA

This dish was a Sam Henderson production, and it was a great combination of textures. We corned beef cheeks, cooked them sous vide, and turned them into a terrine that we cut into cubes. Then we cooked beef tendon, puréed it with a little banana for sweetness, and turned it into what we called a veil; it was like a beefy slice of melted American cheese. The puffed tendon was the best part. We might not have been the first ones to puff a beef tendon, but we certainly devoted a lot of time and energy to perfecting the process.

Getting the puffs to work was all about drying the tendon correctly. That's always the key to puffing things: controlling the moisture content. Puffing happens when you put an ingredient with some water content into oil, and that water heats up and wants to escape the oil in the form of steam; in doing so, it creates a puff. Sam eventually figured out that if she ground the tendon first and then dried it, the puff would be even lighter and lacier.

SERVES 6

Cheek Terrine (page 262)

Banana-Tendon "Veil" (page 262)

Puffed Beef Tendons (page 263)

Banana-Horseradish Sauce (page 263)

Myoga Pickle (page 263)

Pickled young juniper berries

Bay Leaf Powder (page 262)

1. Gently warm the cheek terrine in a low oven with some of its braising liquid.

2. For each serving, place 1 portion of the cheek terrine on a plate and lay 1 portion of the veil over the top. Brûlé with a blowtorch until there is a little char and the corners have melted. Garnish with a puffed beef tendon, a quenelle of banana-horseradish, 2 myoga petals, and 2 juniper berries. Dust with bay leaf powder.

CHEEK TERRINE

600 grams picked Corned Beef Cheeks (recipe follows)

5 grams Bay Leaf Powder (page 236)

60 grams braising liquid reserved from Corned Beef Cheeks

Kosher salt

1. While still warm, combine the picked beef cheeks, bay leaf powder, and braising liquid. Season with salt. Pack the mixture into a one-sixth pan (7 x 6 inches), cover with plastic wrap, and weigh down for several hours.
2. Once cool, cut the terrine into six to eight ⅓-inch-thick portions roughly 2 x 2½ inches.

CORNED BEEF CHEEKS

1 kilogram beef cheeks, cleaned of sinew, glands, and blood

25 grams kosher salt

20 grams sugar

3.75 grams Instacure #1

945 grams water

10 juniper berries, toasted

1 bay leaf

125 grams chicken or beef stock

25 grams duck fat

1. In a large container, combine the cheeks with the salt, sugar, Instacure, water, juniper berries, and bay leaf. Refrigerate for 24 hours. Reserving the brine, rinse the beef cheeks and pat dry.
2. Weigh the beef cheeks and portion out 600 grams. Vacuum-seal the beef cheeks, stock, duck fat, and 50 milliliters of the brine in a cryovac bag. Cook sous vide in a 176°C water bath for 15 hours.

3. While still warm, pick the meat as you would pulled pork, taking care to discard any remaining sinew. Reserve the braising liquid for the terraine.

BANANA-TENDON "VEIL"

100 grams Cooked Beef Tendon (recipe follows), cubed

200 grams banana juice (we used Looza brand)

8 grams horseradish, grated or finely chopped

0.5 gram grated lemon zest

5 grams lemon juice

Kosher salt

Cooking spray

1. Melt the beef tendons in the microwave with a few splashes of water, about 2 minutes on medium power.
2. In a small saucepan, bring the banana juice to about 160°F over high heat.
3. In a blender, blend the tendons, banana juice, horseradish, lemon zest, and lemon juice until smooth. Season with salt and pass through a chinois.
4. Cut two sheets of acetate to fit a half-sheet pan. Coat the acetate with cooking spray. Using an offset spatula, spread the sauce on one of the sheets to about ⅛ inch thick. Top with the second sheet of acetate. Let cool.
5. Peel off the acetate and slice the tendon into 2½ x 3½-inch rectangles. Store between small sheets of parchment and refrigerate until ready to use.

COOKED BEEF TENDON

500 grams beef tendons

Kosher salt

6 sprigs thyme

1 bay leaf

4 cloves garlic

Season the tendons lightly with salt. Put the thyme, bay leaf, and garlic in a sachet. Vacuum-seal the tendons and sachet in a cryovac bag. Cook sous vide in a 194°F water bath for 15 hours. Drain and cool the cooked tendons.

PUFFED BEEF TENDONS

400 grams Cooked Beef Tendon (above)

Neutral oil, for deep-frying

1. Pass the tendons through a meat grinder on a medium die. Spread the ground tendons in a single layer over parchment and dry overnight in the oven with only the pilot light on. Once the tendons are dry and brittle, break into rough pieces, about 2 x 2 inches.
2. Heat a pot of oil to 375°F.
3. Deep-fry the tendons until puffy, about 30 seconds. Pat down on paper towels.

BANANA-HORSERADISH SAUCE

525 grams banana juice (we used Looza brand)

2 grams grated lemon zest

18 grams lemon juice

40 grams fresh horseradish, grated or finely chopped

4.5 grams agar

Kosher salt

1. In a small blender, blend the banana juice, lemon zest, lemon juice, and horseradish until smooth. Shear in the agar, then pass the mixture through a chinois into a saucepan.
2. Bring the mixture to a boil over high heat. Cook for 5 minutes, then pour into a one-sixth pan. Cool in an ice bath.
3. When cool, blend the mixture once more and pass through a chinois. Season with salt to taste. Refrigerate until ready to use.

MYOGA PICKLE

1 bulb myoga ginger, root trimmed, separated into petals

75 grams red wine vinegar

75 grams verjus

75 grams beet juice

Place the myoga petals in a large bowl. In a saucepan, bring the vinegar and verjus to a boil, then pour over the petals. Add the beet juice. Refrigerate for at least 24 hours before serving.

ALDER BURGER

We never served a burger at wd~50, but I came up with my take on burgers there and served them at occasional events before I eventually put them on the menu at Alder.

The first step was figuring out the meat blend: Ground chuck and ground round are both excellent cuts for flavor, as is sirloin. I like a blend of 80 percent chuck or round to 20 percent sirloin. The other key factors are fat content (15 to 20 percent yields maximum flavor) and salt. Salt is vital to the structure of a meatball, meat loaf, or burger patty: In addition to seasoning the meat, it roughs up the proteins, allowing them to bind together. We also added milk powder to our patties for structure—a classic commercial sausage-making move that Mike Sheerin taught me.

SERVES 8

825 grams chuck steak, preferably wagyu, cut into 1-inch chunks

540 grams boneless short rib, cut into 1-inch chunks

Shio Kombu (page 268)

70 grams nonfat milk powder

385 grams kosher salt

8 slices American Cheese à la wd~50 (page 268)

8 burger buns (preferably Martin's potato rolls), toasted

8 half-sour pickle spears

Sliced onion

Ketchup

1. Toss the chuck steak and short rib with the minced shio kombu, milk powder, and salt. Pass through a meat grinder using a medium die. (In a pinch, you could do this in a food processor—just don't pulse it to a paste.) Refrigerate for 8 hours or up to overnight. (This resting time helps the umami flavor of the seaweed work its way into the burger meat.) Form into 8 burger patties.

2. Sear the burgers on a scorching hot griddle; brown the outside quickly and keep the inside nice and rare. Put the cheese on the patties to melt a bit before removing them from the griddle. Let the burgers rest a minute or two before putting them between toasted buns. Serve the pickles on the side with sliced onion and ketchup.

SHIO KOMBU

Wrapping a piece of meat in kombu is a well-established Japanese method of imparting tons of umami to protein. After going to a kombu factory and seeing *shio kombu* made in Japan, I wanted to make my own. We stuck with the classic method of making it, but we then used it to season dishes that were not traditionally Japanese, like burgers and compound butters.

100 grams shredded kombu/kombu strips

80 grams soy sauce

45 grams rice vinegar

70 grams sake

25 grams mirin

30 grams sugar

Rinse the kombu, place it in a saucepan, and cover with hot tap water; let sit for 30 minutes to rehydrate. Drain off the water and add the remaining ingredients to the pot. Cook over medium heat until the kombu is super tender, about 1 hour. If the liquids boil off, replenish the water. Cool completely, then mince.

AMERICAN CHEESE À LA WD~50

American cheese is my guilty pleasure. When I worked at Prime in Las Vegas, I used to spoon some of our beef tartare onto a slice of American cheese, fold it, and eat it like a taco. All the cooks made fun of me for that.

I eat way more American cheese than the average American, so it was only a matter of time before I decided to make my own version of it. The problem with melting different types of cheese together (in this case, American and cheddar) is that cheeses melt differently, so they tend to separate in the same pot. To resolve that, we added sodium citrate (a key ingredient in Kraft singles), which helps cheese melt more

effectively. And we added carrageenan, a stabilizing agent derived from seaweed, to give the cheese enough structure to be sliced. Incidentally, you can add Velveeta, a carrageenan-stabilized cheese, to pretty much anything you're melting and it will help make it creamy and smooth. The same goes for cream cheese: Because it's loaded with gums, it can help pull sauces together. Add some to your next batch of scrambled eggs or mac and cheese.

A note about this cheese: It works best in big batches. If you make a small batch for home use and it's on the soft side, just throw it in the freezer for 15 minutes before slicing it.

3 grams kosher salt

10 grams sodium citrate

4 grams iota carrageenan

1 gram kappa carrageenan

170 grams beer (ideally a pilsner ale)

200 grams cheddar cheese, grated

80 grams American cheese, grated

1. In a saucepan, shear the dry ingredients into the beer. Bring the solution to a very low simmer (it needs to reach 180°F for the carrageenans to hydrate).

2. Gradually add the grated cheeses, stirring off the heat until everything is fully incorporated. If too much liquid evaporates, the hydrocolloids (carrageenans) will make the mixture grainy. If that happens, a quick fix is to splash a couple of extra tablespoons of beer into the mix to loosen it up. Pour into a round container that's roughly the diameter you'll want the cheese slices to be. Refrigerate until set, at least 2 hours.

3. Remove from the mold and slice (using an old-fashioned wire cutter, or even a guitar string, is best). Store between pieces of waxed paper.

DESSERT

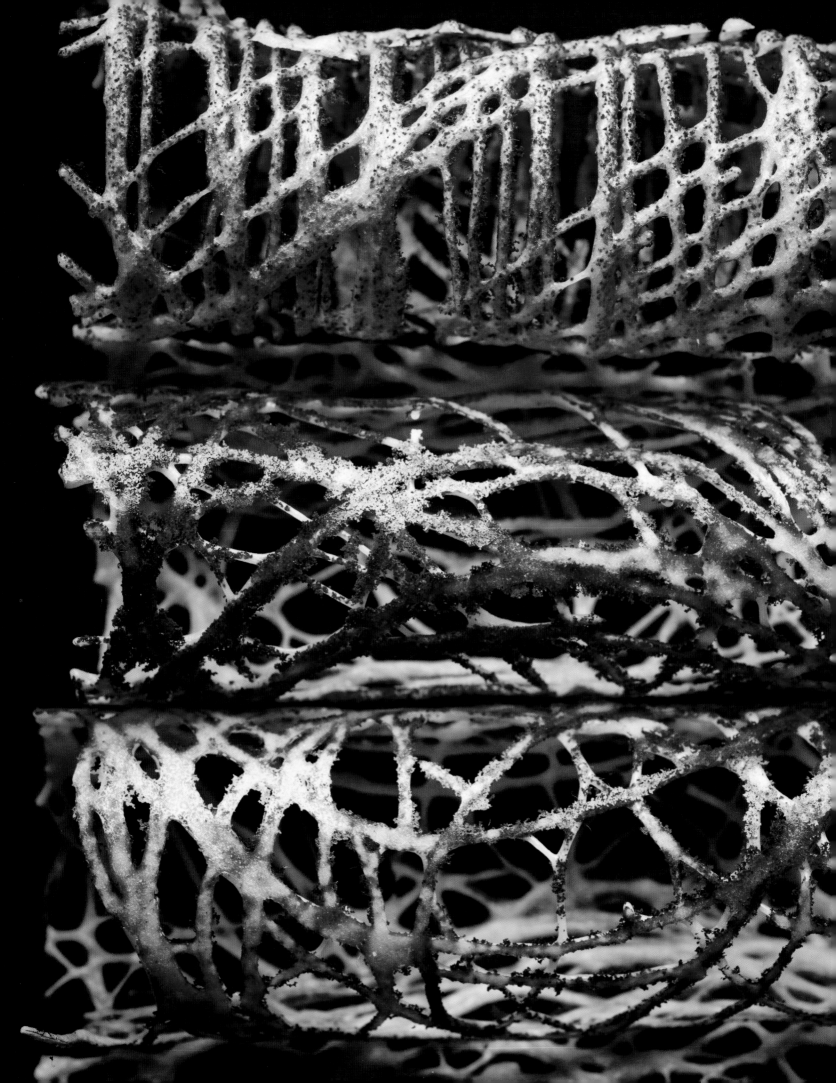

When I opened wd~50, I wanted Sam Mason to be the pastry chef. Never mind that Sam had other ideas—like getting out of the fine-dining game for good. I knew Sam from our brief time together at Palladin, and his desserts at Union Pacific were showstoppers. (The best photo in the Union Pacific cookbook is a shot of Sam's panna cotta with popcorn. Back then, people thought that was crazy.)

Sam and I had a couple of long conversations, and I finally talked him into coming to wd~50. He was the perfect fit: He was full of great ideas, but he was also old-school. He could make a proper crème brûlée, and bake a cookie that any grandma would appreciate. He's also the ice cream whisperer. Nobody makes ice cream as well as Sam Mason does—watching him make it is like watching Michael Jordan do a layup. It's effortless. Sam would make ice

cream out of flavors that had no business being in ice cream—Manchego, chorizo—but they were so good, none of us questioned them.

People still talk mythically about Sam's desserts at wd~50. By the fourth year of wd~50, though, Sam felt it was time to go. He left to open a bar, Lady Jay's; then he went on to open a mayonnaise company and a successful ice cream business, Odd Fellows.

Some people think that I poached Sam's replacement, Alex Stupak, from Grant Achatz—chef/owner of the renowned restaurant Alinea in Chicago—but the truth is, Alex sent me a letter saying he was interested in the job.

When he arrived, his desserts were great, but they felt more Alinea than wd~50: extremely precise, technical, intricate, flawless—and a little sweeter than I liked. There's a learning curve for any chef who comes from a restaurant with a strong identity. You have to unlearn some things. And you have to make sure you make your own mark. Alex respected Sam but he wanted to stand out for his own ideas, and he worked like mad to make that happen.

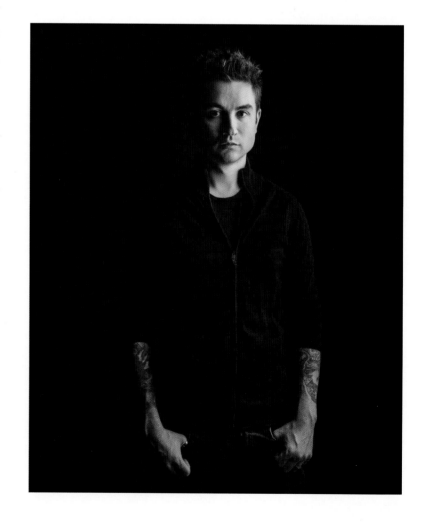

Alex and I were constantly bouncing concepts around, and as a result, he really helped push wd~50 forward. He did a lot of cool stuff with dehydrating and with gums (see the tart with the false shell on page 291), and he developed a distinct plating style. The double quenelle—two stacked on top of each other—is signature Stupak. By the time he left wd~50 in 2010, he was truly one of the best pastry chefs on earth. Unbeknownst to many at the time, Alex had a burning desire to bring his version of Mexican food to New York. He now owns multiple successful Mexican restaurants, including Empellón Taqueria, Al Pastor, and Cocina.

Alex proposed Malcolm Livingston II, one of the pastry cooks, as his replacement. Before he came to wd~50, Malcolm was working at Per Se and staging every Sunday with Alex. When Malcolm stepped up to the lead role, he was on a bigger learning curve than Sam or Alex

had been. He was really good at classical desserts—he had more classical training than Alex—but he hadn't been on his own, experimenting with new techniques, in the way his predecessors had. He arrived with an eagerness to prove himself, though, and he created a suite of desserts that had their own personality, that delivered the right balance of innovation and pleasure, and that helped establish him as a force in the industry. I couldn't have been happier when René Redzepi offered Malcolm the opportunity to become pastry chef at Noma when we announced that wd~50 was closing. As a chef, one of the things you want most is to see the staff move on to great jobs and represent you well—and Malcolm has done that.

FRENCH TOAST, BROWN BUTTER ICE CREAM, RAISIN PURÉE

One of Sam Mason's greatest hits. There's great technique behind the dish, and the composition is gorgeous, but when you eat it, all you can think about is a piece of warm cinnamon-raisin bread slathered in butter, and you just want more. Sam had a knack for knowing the possibilities and limitations of an ingredient, and this was a dish that showcased both his creativity and his restraint.

SERVES 12

Raisin Purée (page 278)

Brioche Toast (page 278)

Raisin Paper (page 278)

Brown Butter Ice Cream (page 278)

Maple Gel (page 279)

Bacon Bits (page 279)

Put a good dollop of raisin purée on each plate, then use a palette knife to smear it across the plate. Starting from the crest of the smear, line up your components: toast, a wafer of raisin paper standing up next to it, a quenelle of ice cream on the other side of the paper. Add a smallish dollop of maple gel (drag it, too) and a sprinkle of bacon.

RAISIN PURÉE

400 grams raisins
225 grams water
4 grams ground cinnamon

1. Combine the raisins and water in a saucepan and bring to a boil over high heat. Cook, uncovered, until the mixture is almost dry.
2. Transfer the mixture to a blender and process until smooth. Add the cinnamon and blend until combined. Refrigerate until ready to use.

RAISIN PAPER

450 grams raisins, soaked overnight in cold water
   and drained
1 egg white

1. Heat the oven to 200°F.
2. In a blender, process the soaked raisins until smooth. Add the egg white and blend until combined.
3. Pour the mixture onto a sheet pan and spread into a thin, even layer. Bake for 2 hours, until dry. Let cool, then break into pieces.

BRIOCHE TOAST

1 loaf Brioche (page 236)
1 kilogram milk
60 grams rum
225 grams powdered sugar
4 grams ground cinnamon
1 gram grated nutmeg
4 eggs
112 grams clarified butter

1. Slice the brioche into bricks that are 2 inches long and 1 inch thick. Set aside.
2. In a large bowl, combine the milk, rum, sugar, cinnamon, nutmeg, and eggs. Fold in the brioche bricks and soak for 20 minutes.
3. In a sauté pan, heat 14 grams of the clarified butter over medium heat. Being careful not to crowd the pan, panfry the brioche pieces until golden, about 2 minutes. Set aside on a sheet pan lined with paper towels. Repeat for the remaining brioche, adding more clarified butter to the pan as needed. (You may not use all the butter.)

BROWN BUTTER ICE CREAM

910 grams butter
1 kilogram whole milk
90 grams nonfat milk powder
115 grams sugar
32 grams Trimoline
150 grams glucose powder
150 grams eggs
225 grams heavy cream

1. In a large saucepan, melt the butter over medium heat. Cook until browned and nutty, at least 5 minutes. Carefully whisk in the milk (the mixture may splatter). Cover and refrigerate overnight.
2. The next morning, pierce the butter—it should have solidified—and strain out 1 quart of brown milk. (Reserve the butter for other uses.)
3. In a large saucepan, combine the brown milk and milk powder and bring to a simmer over medium heat. Add the sugar, Trimoline, and glucose and bring the mixture to a boil.
4. Meanwhile, place the eggs in a large bowl. In a slow, steady stream, whisk the sugar-milk mixture into the eggs, then whisk in the cream. Chill over an ice bath.

5. Churn the mixture in an ice cream maker according to the manufacturer's instructions. Freeze until ready to use.

MAPLE GEL

3 grams low-acyl gellan gum
250 grams cold water
50 grams maple syrup

1. Hydrate the gellan in the cold water. Pour the mixture into a blender.
2. In a small saucepan, bring the maple syrup to a boil over high heat. Pour into the blender and blend to combine. Cool over an ice bath.

BACON BITS

2 slices bacon

Heat a pan over medium heat and add the bacon. Fry until crispy and chop into small pieces.

CRÈME BRÛLÉE PEARLS

Another Sam Mason update of a classic dessert.

SERVES 4

Crème Brûlée Tubes (page 284)
Cocoa Caramel (page 284), some set and
  some warm

Crème Brûlée Pearls (page 284)
Micro arugula
Orange zest

1. Unmold the crème brûlée tubes and cut them into 2-inch lengths. Arrange them on a sizzle plate and cover with piece of the set caramel. Flash gently under a hot broiler until the caramel is melted.

2. Transfer the carameled crème brûlée tube to a plate. Dribble a dot or two of the caramel on the plate. Flank the tube with little piles of pearls. Nestle a sprig of micro arugula in the pearls, and garnish with a flick or two of microplaned orange zest. Serve immediately.

CRÈME BRÛLÉE TUBES

325 grams Crème Brûlée Base (recipe follows)

Fill flexible pastry tubes—either silicone or the plastic ones you get frozen ice in in the summer—with the mixture while it is still warm and leave to set in the refrigerator.

CRÈME BRÛLÉE BASE

1,000 grams cream

230 grams sugar

10 grams vanilla beans

322 grams pasteurized egg yolks

300 grams water

4.15 grams agar

0.6 grams locust bean gum

1. In a saucepan over medium heat, combine the cream, sugar, and vanilla and heat until warm to the touch. Remove from the heat and let steep for 20 minutes.
2. Temper the hot cream mixture into the egg yolks, gently whisking but not aerating. Measure out 650 grams of this egg-cream mixture.
3. Combine the water, agar, and locust bean gum in a blender and process for 1 minute. Transfer the mixture to a small saucepan and bring to 175°F for 3 minutes to hydrate. Gently whisk into the egg-cream mixture while still hot. Cool.

COCOA CARAMEL

200 grams superfine sugar

120 grams glucose

2 tablespoons cocoa powder

150 milliliters water

1. Combine the sugar and glucose in a saucepan and set over medium heat. Let cook, undisturbed, until golden brown.
2. In a medium bowl, whisk the cocoa and water until combined.
3. Remove the caramel from the heat, and whisk in the cocoa water. Pour half of the mixture onto a sheet pan, reserving the other half. Place the sheet pan in the refrigerator until the caramel has set. Warm the other half of the caramel when ready to serve.

CRÈME BRÛLÉE PEARLS

500 grams vegetable oil

325 grams Crème Brûlée Base (left)

1. Freeze the oil overnight. Let warm to 50°F.
2. Warm the crème brûlée base until it's hot to the touch and transfer it to a squeeze bottle. Drop pearls of the mixture into the vegetable oil, where they will take shape. Let set for 4 minutes.
3. Use a skimmer to remove the pearls, and rinse under warm water. Refrigerate until ready to use.

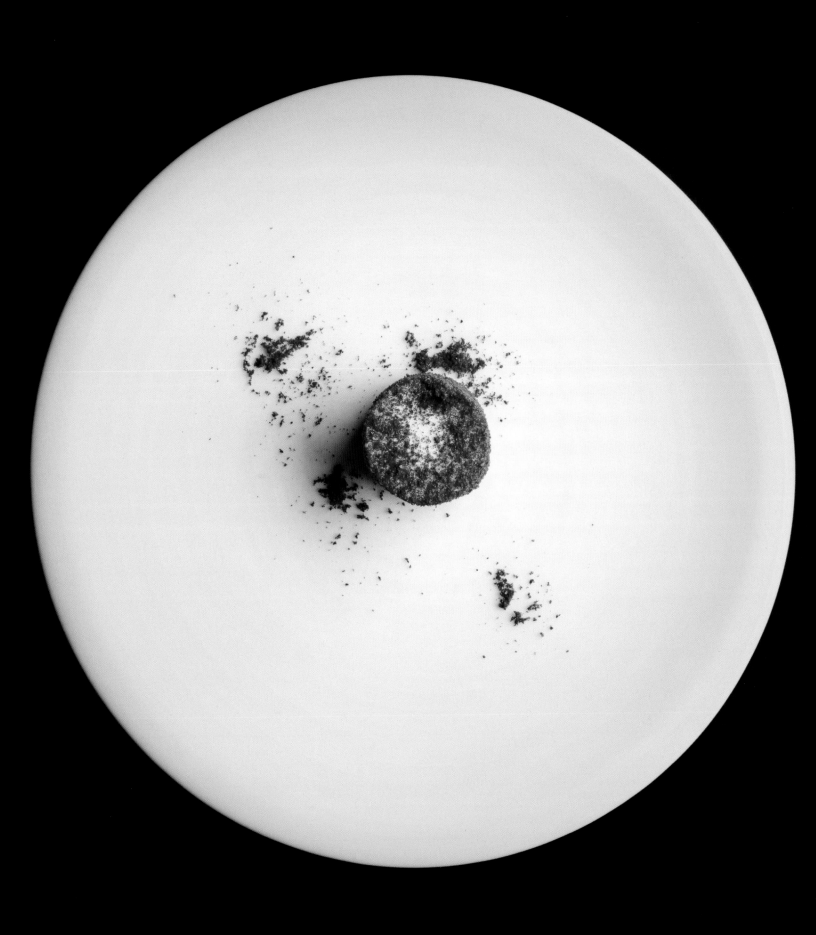

VANILLA ICE CREAM, RASPBERRY

This Alex Stupak dessert was similar to the liquid-filled foie gras cylinder that sometimes preceded it on the menu. It was a stunning twist on a simple flavor combination of vanilla ice cream with balsamic vinegar and raspberries.

SERVES 10

Balsamic Centers (page 288)   **Raspberry Streusel (page 288)**
Vanilla Ice Cream (page 288)

1. Cut acetate sheets into 10 strips, 1¼ x 4 inches. Wrap the bottoms of ten 1½-inch-diameter, 1-inch-deep ring molds with plastic wrap (this will be the "base" of the mold). Line each mold with an acetate strip. The strip will extend up over the mold.

2. Fill 10 cavities of a ½-inch demisphere silicone mold with the balsamic mixture. Freeze the mold in liquid nitrogen to solidify the balsamic mixture.

3. Fill a pastry bag with the vanilla ice cream. Pipe the vanilla ice cream into the lined ring molds to fill them.

4. Remove the frozen balsamic centers from the demisphere mold and push one into the center of each ice cream–filled ring mold. Level the ice cream in each mold using a small offset spatula and freeze for at least 6 hours.

5. Remove the ice cream from the ring molds and roll in the raspberry streusel. Serve immediately.

BALSAMIC CENTERS

500 grams balsamic vinegar

0.5 gram xanthan gum

325 grams glucose powder

100 grams sugar

80 grams grappa

In a blender, process the balsamic and xanthan gum until smooth. Pour into a bowl and whisk in the remaining ingredients. Refrigerate until ready to use.

VANILLA ICE CREAM

900 grams whole milk

404 grams heavy cream

270 grams egg yolks

275 grams sugar

81 grams nonfat milk powder

154 grams glucose powder

1 vanilla bean, split

6 grams guar gum

6 grams kosher salt

1. In a large saucepan, bring the milk and cream to a boil over high heat.
2. In a large bowl, whisk together the egg yolks and sugar. Temper the yolk mixture with the warm milk mixture, then pour into a blender. Add the milk powder, glucose powder, vanilla seeds, guar gum, and salt and purée until smooth. Strain through a chinois and chill over an ice bath.
3. Churn the mixture in an ice cream machine according to the manufacturer's instructions. Freeze until ready to use.

RASPBERRY STREUSEL

360 grams all-purpose flour

220 grams almond flour

300 grams sugar

320 grams butter

10 grams kosher salt

450 grams freeze-dried raspberries

1. Heat the oven to 300°F.
2. In a food processor, combine the all-purpose flour, almond flour, and sugar. Add the butter and salt and blend until the mixture becomes mealy. Spread the mixture out on a parchment-lined sheet pan and bake for 30 minutes. Let cool.
3. Return the cooled mixture to the food processor along with the freeze-dried raspberries and blend until combined. Store in an airtight container at room temperature until ready to use.

PASSION FRUIT "TART," SESAME, ARGAN OIL, MERINGUE

When you dig into this tart, you're prepared for the crust to respond to your fork like crust usually does, but it's all the same texture. When I was thinking of which flavors to use for this, I wanted to find a flavor combination people hadn't tried. Peanut butter and jelly work together. Why? Think about peanut butter: It's nutty, it's salty, and it's sweet. Jelly: It's fruity, it's sweet, and it's acidic. Start with two columns and write down everything you can think of that fits into those categories. Based on that idea, passion fruit and argan oil should work. Or black currant and black sesame. You can deliver something that is seemingly new but that's based on the basic principle of peanut butter and jelly.

—Alex Stupak

SERVES 10

Passion Fruit "Tarts" (page 292)   Black Sesame Sauce (page 294)
Meringue (page 294)   Sesame Seed Sable (page 295)
Argan oil   Black Sesame Powder (page 295)
Passion Fruit Sauce (page 294)

1. Remove the plated "tarts" from the refrigerator.

2. Transfer the meringue to a pastry bag fitted with a straight tip and pipe 5 or 6 mounds of meringue on and beside each tart. Brown the meringue with a blowtorch.

3. Drizzle argan oil around each tart. Place some small pools of passion fruit sauce directly in the argan oil. Apply some black sesame sauce to each plate. Place some shards of sesame seed sable beside the tart and the meringue. Sprinkle some black sesame powder on each plate and serve immediately.

PASSION FRUIT "TARTS"

Tahini Gel (recipe follows)
Passion Fruit Curd (recipe follows)
Meringue (page 294)

1. Line a half-sheet pan with a silicone baking mat. Spread with a thin, even layer of tahini gel.
2. Cut a sheet of acetate into ten ½ x 9-inch strips. Lay out rows of acetate strips on a clean silicone baking mat. Carefully spread a thin, even layer of tahini gel over the acetate strips.
3. Lift an acetate strip from the baking mat and carefully pinch the two ends together to form a circle. Secure with tape.
4. Place the acetate ring on the silicone mat that's lined with tahini gel, running your finger around the top of the ring to press into place and remove any excess gel. Repeat this process with the remaining acetate strips. Transfer the false tart shells to the freezer until frozen solid.
5. Remove the tart shells from the freezer. Transfer the passion fruit curd into a sauce funnel and dispense into each of the false tart shells. Return the tarts to the freezer for 6 hours.
6. Lay out 10 plates. Remove the tarts from the freezer. Carefully peel away the tape and all of the acetate. Quickly place a tart in the center of each plate and store the plates in the refrigerator.

TAHINI GEL

8 grams agar
750 grams water
8 grams xanthan gum
2 sheets silver gelatin, bloomed in ice water
750 grams tahini
100 grams brown sugar
5 grams kosher salt

1. In a large saucepan, bring the agar and water to a boil. Cook for 1 minute, then transfer to a small blender. Shear in the xanthan gum and bloomed gelatin, then blend in the tahini, brown sugar, and salt. Set the gel over an ice bath and let cool.
2. Blend the mixture until smooth, then strain through a tamis. Refrigerate until ready to use.

PASSION FRUIT CURD

120 grams passion fruit juice
15 grams yuzu juice
0.5 gram agar
135 grams eggs
130 grams sugar
0.5 gram citric acid
0.5 gram kosher salt
175 grams butter

1. In a large pot, bring the passion fruit juice, yuzu juice, and agar to a boil, about 1 minute.
2. In a separate bowl, whisk the eggs and the sugar. Temper the eggs with the hot juice mixture, then return the mixture to the pot.
3. Place the pot over medium-high heat and bring to 173°F.
4. Pour the mixture into a small blender and on low speed, mix in the citric acid, salt, and butter. Refrigerate until ready to use.

MERINGUE

190 grams sugar

125 grams egg whites

1 gram citric acid

In a double boiler over low heat, whisk the sugar and egg whites until the sugar dissolves and the mixture reaches 150°F. Pour into a stand mixer and whip to medium-stiff peaks. Whisk in the citric acid. Refrigerate until ready to use, and rewhip as needed.

PASSION FRUIT SAUCE

250 grams passion fruit juice

1.25 grams xanthan gum

In a blender, process the juice and xanthan gum on high for 3 minutes. Transfer the mixture to a squeeze bottle. Refrigerate until ready to use.

BLACK SESAME SAUCE

250 grams water

4 grams agar

250 grams black sesame seeds, soaked in water for 12 hours and then drained

200 grams honey

50 grams virgin sesame oil

5 grams kosher salt

1. Bring the water and agar to a boil. Transfer to a blender along with the sesame seeds and purée until extremely smooth. Add the honey, sesame oil, and salt and continue to blend until homogenous.
2. Pass the mixture through a chinois and cool in an ice bath. Refrigerate for 1 hour.
3. Return the mixture to the blender and purée until smooth. Pass through a chinois again and transfer to a squeeze bottle. Refrigerate until ready to use.

SESAME SEED SABLE

200 grams sugar

6 grams kosher salt

275 grams all-purpose flour

250 grams almond flour

250 grams white sesame seeds

300 grams butter, at room temperature

1 vanilla bean, split

1. In a bowl, whisk together the sugar, salt, all-purpose flour, almond flour, and sesame seeds.
2. In a stand mixer fitted with the paddle attachment, beat the butter and vanilla seeds until fluffy, about 4 minutes.
3. Scrape down the sides of the bowl, then add the dry ingredients in two additions.

4. Place a sheet of parchment paper on a flat surface and turn the dough out on top. Place another sheet of parchment paper on top of the dough. Roll out the dough to ¼ inch thick and freeze for at least 4 hours.
5. Heat the oven to 350°F.
6. Remove the top sheet of parchment and bake the sable until golden brown, about 18 minutes. Let cool. Break into small irregular shards and store in an airtight container until ready to use.

BLACK SESAME POWDER

452 grams black sesame seeds
104 grams N-Zorbit
104 grams sugar
6 grams kosher salt

In a food processor, combine the sesame seeds, salt, and sugar with the N-Zorbit. Process into a fine powder.

KAFFIR LIME LEAF CHURROS

Mignardises were always my favorite part of the dessert program because I could steal one or two whenever I walked by. I'm pretty sure that when Malcolm Livingston made these two favorites—Kaffir Lime Leaf Churros and Root Beer Chews (page 299)—he accounted for this and made enough to cover my take.

SERVES 12

500 grams water

100 grams kaffir lime leaves

85 grams butter

308 grams bread flour

25 grams freeze-dried corn powder

7 grams kosher salt, plus more as needed

2 eggs

Neutral oil, for deep-frying

Sugar

1. Bring the water to a boil, then pour into a small blender. Blend the water and the kaffir lime leaves until smooth. Chill over an ice bath, then strain.

2. In a large saucepan, combine 450 grams of the infusion and the butter, place over high heat, and bring to a boil. Remove from the heat and add the bread flour, corn powder, and salt, taking care to avoid creating lumps. Stir with a spatula until the mixture comes into a ball. Place the pot back over the heat and cook, stirring, for 1 minute.

3. Transfer the dough to a stand mixer fitted with the paddle attachment. Mix on low speed, adding the eggs one at a time until combined. Increase the speed to medium for 1 minute. The dough will be slightly warm.

4. Place the mixture in a pastry bag fitted with a medium star tip. Pipe the churros in a straight line onto a half-sheet pan lined with parchment paper. Freeze.

5. Heat a large pot of oil to 350°F.

6. Cut the churros into desired sizes. (We made them about 6 inches long.) While still frozen, fry the churros until golden brown, 3 to 5 minutes. Roll in sugar, sprinkle with salt, and, if needed, cover with towels and place in a 300°F oven to keep warm. (They will keep for 20 minutes in the oven without drying out.)

ROOT BEER CHEWS

MAKES 35 CHEWS

88 grams glucose syrup

188 grams sugar

200 grams heavy cream

50 grams root beer soda

175 grams frozen black cherry purée (we used Boiron)

3.75 grams agar

5 grams apple pectin

175 grams white chocolate

10 grams silver sheet gelatin, bloomed in ice water

0.5 gram citric acid

0.4 gram root beer flavor

0.2 gram black cherry flavor

1 drop red food coloring

Cooking spray

1. On a sheet pan lined with a silicone baking mat, arrange 4 confectionery rulers that are at least ½ inch high in an 8 x 6-inch rectangle. Secure the outside corners of the rulers with tape.

2. In a large pot, combine the glucose syrup, sugar, cream, root beer soda, and cherry purée. Whisk in the agar and apple pectin. Place over medium heat and cook, whisking, until the mixture reaches 224°F. It should look thick and smooth.

3. Meanwhile, in a microwave-safe bowl or over a double boiler, melt the white chocolate.

4. Whisk the white chocolate, bloomed gelatin, citric acid, root beer flavor, black cherry flavor, and red food coloring into the cherry mixture. Mix thoroughly, using a rubber spatula to combine once the mixture becomes too sticky for the whisk.

5. Pour the mixture into the confection bars and refrigerate for at least 6 hours. The chew is best when cooled overnight.

6. Remove from the fridge and portion into ½-inch cubes. Place on a sheet pan, on a silicone baking mat coated with cooking spray. Wrap the tray in plastic and freeze until ready to serve.

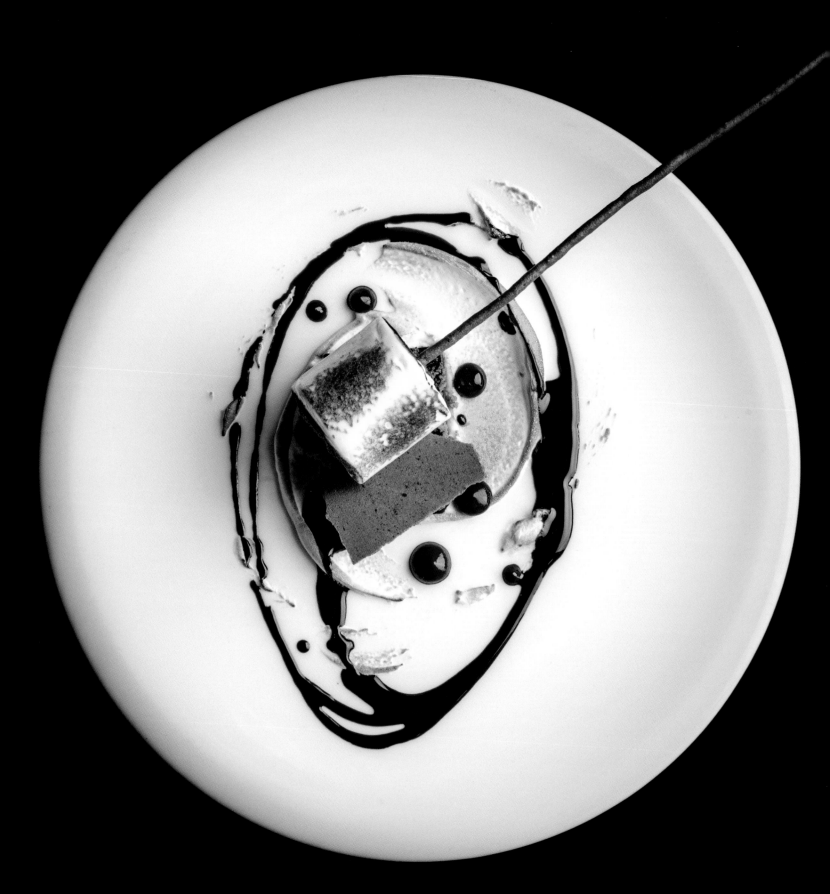

S'MORES, BITTER COCOA, MEZCAL, BLACK CURRANT

Malcolm's version of a s'more looked nothing like the original, but the spirit of the childhood favorite was all there. Instead of burning the marshmallows, he burned the ice cream. In place of the smoke: mezcal in one sauce and chili powder in the other.

SERVES 6

Meringue (page 302)

Bitter Chocolate Sauce (page 302)

Black Currant–Mezcal Sauce (page 302)

6 pieces Graham Crackers (page 302)

6 pieces Ganache Squares (page 303)

6 Meringue Ice Cream "Marshmallows" (page 304)

6 Beer Sticks (page 304)

Crispy Chocolate (page 305)

1. On each plate, with a small offset spatula, spread 2 comet-like schmears of meringue in opposite directions around the diameter of the plate. Char with a blowtorch.

2. Sauce the plate with orbits of bitter chocolate sauce and a few dollops of black currant–mezcal sauce.

3. Lay a graham cracker down and place a piece of ganache on top.

4. Unmold a meringue ice cream "marshmallow" and place on top of the ganache. Char with a blowtorch and pierce with a beer stick. Garnish with crispy chocolate.

MERINGUE

125 grams egg whites

175 grams sugar

1.75 grams citric acid

1. In a double boiler, cook the egg whites with the sugar until the sugar dissolves and the mixture reaches 160°F.
2. Transfer the mixture to a stand mixer fitted with the whisk attachment and whip the meringue into medium-stiff peaks. Add the citric acid and whip for an additional minute on medium speed. Refrigerate, covered, until ready to use.

BITTER CHOCOLATE SAUCE

200 grams water

200 grams sugar

0.5 gram ground Kashmiri chile

2.5 grams kosher salt

50 grams cocoa powder

50 grams Valrhona 70% chocolate

1. In a medium saucepan, combine the water, sugar, chile, and salt and bring to a boil over medium-high heat. Reduce the heat to low and whisk in the cocoa powder and chocolate until completely dissolved.
2. Strain the sauce through a fine chinois. Chill over an ice bath. Set aside.

BLACK CURRANT– MEZCAL SAUCE

50 grams water

8 grams agar

200 grams mezcal (we used Ilegal)

550 grams black currant purée (we used Boiron)

40 grams glucose syrup

3 grams kosher salt

Grated zest of 1 lime

Lime juice, if needed

1. In a medium saucepan, combine the water and agar. Whisk in the mezcal and black currant purée and place over high heat. Bring to a boil, stirring constantly, for 2 minutes. Add the glucose and salt, remove from the heat, and cool the mixture over an ice bath.
2. Once solidified, transfer the mixture to a small blender and add the lime zest. Process until smooth, then pass through a fine chinois. Season the sauce with lime juice, if needed. Refrigerate until ready to use.

GRAHAM CRACKERS

100 grams all-purpose flour

70 grams whole wheat flour

70 grams cake flour

5 grams ground cinnamon

0.75 gram baking soda

2.5 grams kosher salt

160 grams butter

70 grams dark brown sugar

55 grams granulated sugar

20 grams honey

1. Heat the oven to 350°F.
2. In a large bowl, combine the all-purpose flour, whole wheat flour, cake flour, cinnamon, baking soda, and salt.
3. In a stand mixer fitted with the paddle attachment, cream the butter, dark brown sugar, granulated sugar, and honey until smooth and fluffy. Add the dry ingredients in three additions, scraping down the sides of the bowl.
4. Place a sheet of parchment paper on a flat surface and turn the dough out on top. Place another sheet of parchment paper on top of the dough. Roll out the dough to ¼ inch thick.
5. Transfer the dough to a dough sheet and bake for 10 to 20 minutes, depending on the size of the dough sheet. While still hot, use a bicycle pastry cutter to cut the dough into 2-inch squares. Reserve the trimmings to grind into crumbs.

GANACHE SQUARES

45 grams water
1.75 grams agar
85 grams glucose syrup
750 grams heavy cream
315 grams Valrhona 70% chocolate
4 grams kosher salt
1 sheet silver gelatin, bloomed in cold water
Cooking spray

1. In a medium saucepan, whisk together the water, agar, and glucose syrup and bring to a boil over high heat, whisking constantly. Cook for 1 minute, still whisking, then add half of the cream. Whisk lightly and adjust the heat to keep the mixture at a boil. Add the remaining cream and bring the mixture back to a boil.
2. In a small blender, combine the chocolate, salt, and gelatin. Pour the hot cream mixture over the top of the chocolate and blend on the lowest speed until combined. Strain the ganache through a fine chinois.
3. Coat a white plastic deli tray with cooking spray and wipe off with a clean cloth. Measure 700 grams of the ganache and pour onto the tray. Tap out any air bubbles and place in the refrigerator.
4. Once the ganache is set, portion it into 2-inch squares. Refrigerate until ready to use.

MERINGUE ICE CREAM "MARSHMALLOWS"

FLUFF CENTERS
400 grams glucose syrup
200 grams water
3 grams iota carrageenan
3 grams guar gum
5 grams Versawhip
0.1 gram calcium lactate

MERINGUE ICE CREAM
415 grams water
6 grams low-acyl gellan gum
315 grams egg whites
130 grams sugar
50 grams dextrose powder
17.5 grams glucose powder
30 grams nonfat milk powder
80 grams heavy cream
6 grams marshmallow extract
1.5 grams kosher salt

1. Make the fluff centers: Warm the glucose syrup in the microwave. Set aside.
2. In a small pot, bring the water to a boil and pour immediately into a small blender. On the lowest

speed, create a vortex and shear in the iota carrageenan for 1 minute. Add the guar gum, Versawhip, and then the calcium lactate, making sure each gum is thoroughly blended before adding the next. Add the warmed glucose syrup.

3. Turn the blender to high speed and blend for an additional 2 minutes. Cool the mixture over an ice bath. The base will gel slightly as it cools.

4. In a stand mixer fitted with the whisk attachment, whip the cooled base to stiff peaks. It will resemble a shiny meringue. Pipe the fluff into 15 cups of a 1¼-inch-diameter demisphere silicone mold. Transfer to a freezer.

5. Make the meringue ice cream: In a small pot, bring the water to a boil. Pour the water into a blender and blend in the gellan gum on low speed. Turn the blender to high speed and blend for 2 minutes.

6. Meanwhile, in a double boiler, cook the egg whites with the sugar until the sugar dissolves and the mixture reaches 160°F.

7. Stop the blender and pour in the warmed egg white mixture. Blend in the dextrose powder, glucose powder, milk powder, cream, marshmallow extract, and salt. Blend on high speed for about 2 minutes. (Gellan gum is an ionic-dependable gum, which means that you need to add the salt at the final stage—if added earlier, the gel will set too quickly.)

8. Cool the ice cream base over an ice bath. Once it has formed a solid gel, transfer to a blender and reblend until smooth. Pass through a fine-mesh sieve or chinois. Churn the mixture in an ice cream maker according to the manufacturer's instructions.

9. While the ice cream is spinning, prepare the supplies for the ice cream "marshmallow" assembly: You'll need 15 rings of 1¾-inch-diameter PVC pipe cut into 1½-inch lengths and 15 acetate strips cut into strips measuring 1¾ x 6½ inches. Wrap the bottom of the PVC rings with plastic wrap (to form the bottom of the mold) and line the inside of the pipe rings with the acetate strips.

10. Once the ice cream has been spun, transfer it to a pastry bag and pipe it into the prepared molds. Remove the fluff centers from the freezer. Unmold them and push the fluff ½ inch into the centers of the ice cream. Fill the indentation with more ice cream. Using an offset spatula, level the ice cream so it is flat and even. Freeze the molded ice cream until firm, at least 1 hour or until ready to serve.

BEER STICKS

30 grams egg white powder
112 grams powdered sugar
30 grams Ultra-Sperse M
90 grams all-purpose flour
1.5 grams kosher salt
165 grams dark beer

1. Sift together the egg white powder, sugar, Ultra-Sperse, and flour into a stand mixer fitted with the paddle attachment. Add the salt.

2. With the mixer on low speed, slowly stream in the beer to create a lump-free cake batter. Scrape the bottom and sides of the bowl, and re-mix until homogenous. Don't overmix—it will make piping very difficult.

3. Heat a convection oven with a high-speed fan to 300°F.

4. Transfer the dough to a pastry bag with a small tip and pipe long, thin strips (to resemble twigs) onto a parchment-lined sheet pan. Bake until dark but not burned, about 15 minutes. Let cool slightly, then use a palette knife to remove the sticks from the parchment. Trim to about 7 inches long. Let cool completely, then store the sticks in sealed containers in a cool, dry place.

CRISPY CHOCOLATE

150 grams Valrhona 72% chocolate

200 grams egg whites

2.28 grams TicaPAN Quick Crunch

50 grams sugar

60 grams egg yolks

Cooking spray

1. Melt the chocolate in a double boiler or in the microwave. Set aside.
2. In a large bowl, combine the egg whites, quick crunch, and sugar. Using an immersion blender, blend until homogenous. Transfer the mixture to a stand mixer fitted with the whisk attachment. Whip to medium-stiff peaks.
3. Whisk the egg yolks into the melted chocolate and carefully fold the chocolate mixture into the meringue.
4. Cut an acetate sheet to the size of a dehydrator tray. Set the acetate sheet on a flat surface and coat generously with cooking spray. Rub off the cooking spray with a clean cloth. Stack 8 pieces of painter's tape, on top of one another, on either side of the acetate. Using this stack of tape as a thickness guide, spread a thin layer of chocolate on the acetate. Place in the dehydrator until completely crispy, 4 to 6 hours. Place in a sealed container and store in a cool dry place until ready to use.

THE
BAR

The bar at wd~50 was the first stop for many diners, and some of the best mixologists in the world created cocktails here: Eben Freeman, Troy Arcand, and Tona Palomino in the early years, Kevin Denton in the final stretch, and, of course, Jafrul Shahin (more affectionately known as "Jaffy"), who was a fixture from the first day until the last. These guys created drinks the same way we created dishes—by researching new techniques, pairing unexpected flavors, and collaborating with everyone in the kitchen.

But, as Tona points out, the bar was also notable for its simplest role as a neighborhood gathering place: "Even though we were doing some far-out stuff at wd, our bar still had all the best elements of what makes a bar a home away from home: regulars to anchor us to the neighborhood; crazies who would stop in to break up the routine; and, most important, the conviviality. It was first and foremost a fun place to drink and pour drinks."

The bar progressed in lockstep with the kitchen, borrowing techniques whenever possible. "We learned to clarify liquids first using the gelatin freeze-thaw technique (Concord grape juice), then using agar (pear nectar), and finally using a centrifuge (Nigori sake and soursop nectar)," Tona says. "We mirrored the kitchen's own journey through these various methods. Clarification, viscosification, suspension, carbonation, chlorophyllization— the bar learned and used them all in an effort to keep up and represent the restaurant with the same level of curiosity and ambition."

By the time Kevin Denton came on as bar director in 2011, the bar was truly an offshoot of the kitchen. "My third-grade dreams of becoming a mad scientist seemed so tangible when I arrived," he says. "It was a dream come true to be tinkering with booze, powders, and oddball tools—to be nitro-freezing and centrifuging our way to cocktails instead of just shaking and stirring."

DUCK BLIND

SERVES 1

1.5 ounces blended Scotch

1 ounce amontillado sherry

0.5 ounce Smoked Maple Syrup (recipe follows)

Pimentón Oil (recipe follows)

Cacao Oil (recipe follows)

1. Combine the Scotch, sherry, and maple syrup with ice in a mixing glass and stir until cold. Strain into a chilled cocktail glass.

2. Garnish with "cat eyes": Put three drops of the pimentón oil in a triangle pattern on the surface of the cocktail, then dispense a dot of the cacao oil on the side of each pimentón drop. Serve.

SMOKED MAPLE SYRUP

Maple syrup

Cold-smoke the maple syrup for 45 minutes, or to taste. Cool and reserve; it keeps almost indefinitely. We typically smoked a liter at a time; smaller amounts may take less time to acquire an appealingly smoky flavor.

PIMENTÓN OIL

10 grams pimentón

100 grams grapeseed oil

In a blender, blend together the pimentón and grapeseed oil on high speed for 5 minutes. Fine-strain and transfer to an eyedropper bottle.

CACAO OIL

10 grams cacao nibs

100 grams grapeseed oil

In a blender, blend together the cacao nibs and grapeseed oil on high speed for 3 minutes. Fine-strain and transfer to an eyedropper bottle.

OLD SCHOOL

SERVES 1

2 ounces Peanut Butter–Infused Vodka (recipe
follows)

1 ounce Clarified Concord Grape Juice (recipe
follows)

Combine the vodka and grape juice in an iSi siphon
and carbonate. Pour into a rocks glass over 1 large ice
cube and serve.

PEANUT BUTTER–INFUSED VODKA

Peanut butter
750 milliliters vodka

In a half-sheet pan, spread a ½-inch-thick layer of peanut butter. Add the vodka. Cover with plastic wrap
and store at room temperature for 5 to 7 days. Strain
through cheesecloth into a clean bottle.

CLARIFIED CONCORD GRAPE JUICE

1,000 grams chilled Concord grape juice (we would
typically make it by passing the grapes through
a food mill)

2 grams agar (preferably Telephone Brand)

1. Measure out the cold grape juice and 1.5 grams of
the agar (0.2% of total juice weight).
2. Put the remaining portion of the cold juices into a
large saucepan, stir in the agar, then bring to a boil
while stirring. Simmer for a minute, then whisk in
the remaining juice and continue to whisk as the
mixture heats through—it needs to be above 95°F
for the agar to gel. After a minute, transfer the mixture to a bowl set in an ice bath to set.
3. Once set, break up the agar into "curds." Dump
the curds into a cheesecloth-lined chinois set
over a clean bottle and lift and gently squeeze the
cloth to drain. Twist the cloth to press the juice
out gently and quickly. Don't twist too hard or you
will extrude the agar through the cheesecloth.
4. If there are any agar bits in your clarified grape
juice, strain them out by passing it through a cof-
fee filter. Chill until needed.

TEQUILA PEPINO

WHOLE LOTTA LOVAGE

SERVES 1

- 2 ounces blanco tequila
- 0.5 ounce lime juice
- 0.5 ounce simple syrup
- 3 ounces cucumber juice (cucumbers juiced with the peels on)
- Tajín Clásico Seasoning

Combine the tequila, lime juice, simple syrup, and cucumber juice in a cocktail shaker with ice and shake. Rim a rocks glass with Tajín and fill with ice. Strain the cocktail into the glass and serve.

SERVES 1

- 1 small bunch lovage, plus more for garnish
- 0.5 ounce simple syrup
- 2 ounces London dry gin
- 1 ounce passion fruit purée
- 0.25 ounce lime juice
- Tonic

Muddle the bunch of lovage and simple syrup in a cocktail shaker. Add the gin, passion fruit purée, and lime juice and fill with ice. Shake and fine-strain into a highball glass filled with ice. Top with the tonic and garnish with more lovage leaves.

OLIVER CLOTHESOFF

SERVES 1

3.5 ounces Olive Gin (recipe follows)
1 barspoon Pimentón Oil (page 313)

Combine the olive gin and ice in a cocktail shaker and shake until chilled. Strain into a cocktail glass. Float the pimentón oil in the center of the cocktail. Serve.

OLIVE GIN

MAKES ABOUT 1 LITER

500 grams large pitted green olives
1 liter gin

1. Blanch the olives in a pot of boiling water for 5 minutes. Drain, discard the water, and repeat 3 more times.
2. In a blender, purée the gin and blanched olives until smooth.
3. Following the instructions on your centrifuge, spin the olive mixture at 4,600 rpms for 25 minutes. Strain off the olive fats and gently pour the olive gin into a clean bottle.

THE GRADUATING CLASS FROM NOVEMBER 31, 2014.

SCENES FROM THE RESTAURANT'S CLOSING,
INCLUDING DISASSEMBLING THE INTERIOR AFTER THE AUCTION.

ACKNOWLEDGMENTS

For as long as I can remember, I've wanted to be a professional athlete. I used to think it was because I love playing sports, but ultimately I realized it was because I love being part of a team. wd~50 was the best team I ever played on. Writing a book that captured that spirit also required a tremendous team effort, and there are many people to acknowledge:

To the entire staff at wd~50 over the years: You were a better FOH and kitchen crew than I could have ever dreamed up.

To the many amazing people on the floor over the years: Thank you all for explaining our vision to the customers every night. I know I didn't make it easy.

To the office girls, Griffin and Shari: Thanks for keeping it going behind the scenes.

To the gatekeepers at the door: We started and ended with Scott Mayger, but there were many great people in between.

To the bar crew, Jaffy and Kevin, for keeping us all well lubricated.

To Tona: You wore so many hats over the years, which couldn't have been easy with all that hair.

To Sam Mason, Christina Tosi, Alex Stupak, Malcolm Livingston, and the rest of the sugarplum fairies downstairs in the basement sugar shack.

To Junior Dominguez: You hoisted our world onto your shoulders every day and made it look not only easy but fun. Thank you for the cleanest kitchen ever.

To Mike, Fran, J.J., and Reggie, great cooks and even greater friends.

To Sam Henderson: Neither wd~50 nor this book would have reached such heights without you doing all kinds of heavy lifting. Working in the kitchen with you continues to be one of the most rewarding experiences of my career. Thanks for walking in off the street.

Many great people came through the wd~50 kitchen over the years. Thank you all for what you taught me. It was an honor to work side by side with each and every one of you.

To the Lower East Side, for providing a backdrop for tremendous inspiration.

To all the people who ate at wd~50 over the years: We are extremely grateful.

To Phil and JG: The best partners anyone could ask for. Thank you for keeping the doors open all those years.

To Kim Witherspoon at Inkwell, for taking care of the business side of things.

To Tony Bourdain, for believing in our vision.

To Dave Arnold, for always finding and fixing the right gear.

To the team at Ecco: Thank you to Dan Halpern, for your enthusiasm as a diner and an editor, and for your amazing hair; Suet, for laying it all out so beautifully; and Bridget Read, for your support and seemingly endless patience.

To Eric Medsker, for capturing a time and place with your amazing images.

To Brette Warshaw, for making sense of these recipes.

To Peter Meehan, Thanks for hanging out, listening, telling our story, and letting me shine a flashlight in your eye.

To my family: I don't show my love nearly enough.

Rachael, thanks for being an endless well of support all the way back to the 71 Clinton days.

Mom, truly one of the most creative people I know: Thanks for passing it on.

Pop, you said, "Make a difference." I gave it my best shot.

Sawyer and Ellery: You inspire me every day and make me want to be a better man. I hope I can make you pancakes forever.

Maile, the love of my life: wd~50 is where we met. You supported me every inch of the way at the restaurant. It wouldn't have been possible without you. Thank you for everything, especially for waiting a Wylie.

Cheers. Cheers. Cheers.

—Wylie Dufresne

To Kim Witherspoon and her team at Inkwell, for handling the business. To Uncle Tony, for everything, forever. To Dan Halpern and Bridget Read, for their patience. To Brette Warshaw and Sam Henderson, for forming a recipe Voltron. Truly two bosses. To Ryan Healey, Emily Johnson, Charlotte Goddu, and Jon Heindemause, for various and sundry essential acts of editorial support. To Danny Bowien, for burritos and good vibes. To J.J., for the sass and the cheesesteaks. To the whole wd~50 team, front-and-back-of-house, for the exceptional hospitality over the years, particularly the early days of drinking too much too late at Eben Freeman's bar, and during the closing stretch, when every meal was a joy and a revelation. To Wylie, for the opportunity and access and all the stories that didn't make it. A world of knowledge, plus a lot of English muffins and American cheese. To Eric Medsker, for capturing so much magic in so little time. To Hannah, for putting up with it and me, as usual.

—Peter Meehan

GLOSSARY

AGAR—a gum derived from red seaweeds. It is insoluble in cold water, slowly soluble in hot water, and soluble in boiling water, forming a gel upon cooling. The gels are fairly brittle, setting at 90° to 104°F, melting at 203°F. Typical use levels are 0.1% to 2.0%. Rigid gels form at 0.5%. Agar is excellent for forming fluid gels.

BATTER BIND—a modified food starch derived from corn. It appears as a white to off-white powder, and is often used in batters (in conjunction with more traditional batter ingredients like flour and cornstarch) to provide good adhesion of the coating to meat, poultry, vegetable, or seafood products. In fried or baked products, Batter Bind can improve color, flavor, and crispness, and reduce blistering on the surface.

CALCIUM CHLORIDE—a salt and general purpose food additive with many culinary uses from cheese-making to pickling. It is also a source of calcium ions for reaction with alginate, pectin, and gellan to form gels.

CALCIUM GLUCONATE—a salt that is used as a source of calcium ions for reaction with alginate, pectin, and gellan to form gels. It has a more neutral taste than calcium chloride.

CALCIUM LACTATE—a calcium source derived from lactic acid, which is soluble in warm water. It is a source of calcium ions for reactions with alginate, pectin, and gellan to form gels.

CARRAGEENAN—a gum that is a seaweed extract obtained from red seaweed. It is classified mainly as kappa, iota, and lambda types, which differ in solubility and gelling properties. The kappa and iota types require hot water (above 106°F) for complete solubility and can form thermally reversible gels in the presence of potassium and calcium cations, respectively. The kappa gels are brittle with syneresis, while the iota gels are more elastic without syneresis. The lambda type is cold-water soluble and does not form gels. Kappa and iota carrageenans are very reactive with milk protein products. Carrageenan is used to stabilize milk protein at 0.01% to 0.05% and to form water gels at 0.5% to 1.0%.

CITRIC ACID—an acidulant and antioxidant derived from lemons, limes, and oranges in powdered form. Also known as sour salt.

CRISP COAT—a modified starch that is a blend of high-amylose cornstarch and tapioca dextrin. When incorporated into a batter at low levels, it imparts a smooth, uniform appearance to the fried product and provides a firm, crisp surface.

DEXTROSE POWDER—a powdered sweetener derived from corn. It is also known as glucose. It is often used as a less sweet alternative to sugar.

GELLAN GUM—a gelling agent made from fermenting a particular pond lily. There are two forms of gellan: low acyl and high acyl. The two varieties make gels with different properties. Low acyl forms brittle/firm gels and high acyl makes soft/elastic gels. Both types are very sensitive to the presence of calcium, magnesium, potassium, and sodium. These gelling agents can be used alone or in combination with other products to produce a wide variety of interesting textures. They are extremely effective at low-use levels in forming gels with excellent stability, high strength, heat stable, sparkling clarity, outstanding flavor release, and synergy with other hydrocolloids. Hydration occurs around 195°F, with typical concentration levels from 0.3% to 0.7%.

GLUCOSE POWDER—see *dextrose*.

GLUCOSE SYRUP—a food syrup made from starch that has been broken down by enzymes and modified. It is the liquid form of glucose.

GLYCERIN—an alcohol sugar that is used as a plasticizer. It is 75% as sweet as sugar with a flavor that is slightly bittersweet.

GUAR GUM—a thickening and binding agent made from seeds from a pod that resembles tamarind. It is cold-water soluble with typical concentrations between 0.2% and 0.5% and has excellent synergy with both locust bean and xanthan gums.

INSTACURE #1 AND #2—commercial brands of curing salt.

> Instacure #1 is a standard product used for wet curing. It consists of 93.75% table salt and 6.25% sodium nitrite, along with a pink dye to make sure nobody consumes it by mistake. It is used to help retain color in cured meats.

> Instacure #2 contains 92.75% table salt, 6.25% sodium nitrite, and 1% sodium nitrate. It is typically used for dry-cured products that do not require cooking, smoking, or refrigeration.

ISOMALT—an alcohol sugar made from beets. It offers many of the same structural properties as sugar, but it is 50% to 60% less sweet and more resistant to humidity and crystallization.

KAOLIN—an edible clay.

KONJAC—a gelling agent and thickener derived from a root that resembles taro. It needs to be heated to 195°F to hydrate. Common usage levels are from 0.1% to 1.0%. It has excellent synergy with other gums. Konjac will not form a gel on its own, but it will when combined with xanthan, locust bean, or carrageenan.

LECITHIN—an emulsifier that is now made from soy beans, although it was initially derived from egg yolks, where it is naturally abundant.

LOCUST BEAN GUM—a thickener made from carob seeds. It needs to be heated to 180°F to hydrate. It provides high viscosity. When combined with xanthan gum, it creates a slightly elastic gel. When combined with small amounts of kappa carrageenan or agar, it will make those gels more elastic. Typical usage levels are from 0.1% to 1.0%.

MALTODEXTRIN—a sugar produced from corn that is often used in making tuiles, crisps, and papers, and can also work as a thickener. It can be from 6% to 20% as sweet as sugar.

METHYLCELLULOSE—a gelling agent made from wood pulp. The most interesting property of methylcellulose is that, unlike virtually all other gums, it forms a gel when heated. There are several types of methylcellulose that can form very soft to very firm gels when heated to between 140° and 195°F. When used cold, it can help form and stabilize foams as well. Typical usage levels range from 0.05% to 1.0%.

N-ZORBIT M—a modified starch derived from tapioca. N-Zorbit's low density and large surface area make it ideal for making dry powders and pastes from oils.

PGA (PROPYLENE GLYCOL ALGINATE)—an emulsifier, stabilizer, and thickener derived from kelp.

POTASSIUM CHLORIDE—a gelling agent for certain types of carrageenan oil.

SODIUM ALGINATE—a gelling agent and thickener derived from brown algae. It is cold- and hot-water soluble, producing a range of viscosities. It forms heat-stable gels in the presence of calcium ions. Typical usage levels are from 0.5% to 1.0%.

SODIUM HEXAMETAPHOSPHATE—a sequestrant that helps bind calcium and magnesium ions (which can cause various gums to gel prematurely). It is also used as a melting salt in cheese sauces.

SODIUM BISULFITE—a water-soluble preservative that exists in powdered form. It prevents discoloration, browning, and bacterial growth in fruits and vegetables.

SODIUM CITRATE—a buffer and sequestrant obtained from citric acid. It is also used as a melting salt in cheese sauces.

TICAPAN QUICK CRUNCH—a confectionary product from a company called TIC Gums. It's the stuff that makes that nice shell on your Skittles and M&M's!

TRANSGLUTAMINASE—an enzyme that forms a very strong covalent bond in the presence of lysine and glutamine proteins. Its use is best summarized by its nickname, meat glue. It is commonly used to "glue" two or more pieces of meat, fish, or poultry together and can be utilized to create various shapes that would otherwise be difficult (or impossible) to produce by traditional means. It can glue parts of the same protein together into new shapes and sizes, or it can glue different proteins together. The enzymes will increase their activity with heat, and the bonding process can be sped up by applying heat between 125° and 140°F. It is best to avoid highly acidic environments (pH below 4), as the proteins will not bond at these levels.

Activa is the most readily available brand of transglutaminase. Activa RM is the workhorse of meat glues, while Activa GS is particularly good for making slurries to use on larger formats of meat, fish, or poultry. To use Activa GS you need to shear it into a liquid and then get rid of any air in the slurry. The resulting substance stays liquid for many hours.

TRIMOLINE—an invert sugar obtained from beet and cane sugar syrups. Invert sugar helps to reduce, prevent, or control the buildup of crystallization. It allows baked goods to retain freshness and softness for longer periods of time.

ULTRA-SPERSE—a family of cold-water-swelling modified food starches derived from either waxy

maize (Ultra-Sperse M) or tapioca (Ultra-Sperse 3) that are used as thickeners. They are easily dispersible and impart superior sheen, clarity, smoothness, and mouthfeel to things like sauces, instant pudding, salad dressings, etc. Typical usage levels range from 3.0% to 7.5%.

VERSAWHIP—a soy-based protein that can be used in place of egg albumin or gelatin in making foams. It can be used for hot or cold foams and is extremely stable in low pH solutions. Usage levels range from 0.5% to 1.25%.

XANTHAN GUM—a thickener or stabilizer made from the bacterial fermentation of leafy green vegetables such as cabbage. Xanthan is very stable in a wide range of temperatures, pH, and salt levels. It has great synergy with guar gum and will form a gel when mixed with locust bean gum. Typical usage levels range from 0.05% to 0.5%.

INDEX

Page references in *italics* indicate photographs.

HYATT REGENCY CHESAPEAKE BAY
100 Heron Boulevard
Cambridge, MD 21613
Phone: 410-907-1234
View of the 17th hole, River Marsh Golf Course

9/5/03

Just read the review in the Observer, and I will guarantee WD 50 will go belly-up within a year. You can fool some of the people some of the time, but vomitous culinary inventions won't bring repeat customers - Especially that awful location. It's a slum, you know. Pork belly - what a laugh!

Try painting instead of cooking.

X X

Pub. by Traub Co., 2700 Sisson St., Baltimore, MD 21211 · 1-800-933-2220

NEW YORK NY 100
PM
6 SEP
2003

USA 37

FIRST FLIGHT · WRIGHT BROTHERS · 1903
2003

POSTCARD

Address

Wayne Dufresne
WD 50
50 Clinton St.
NY NY 10002